PLASTIC CANVAS
All-Occasion
Gifts ™

Edited by Laura Scott

HOUSE of
WHITE
BIRCHES
PUBLISHERS
SINCE 1947

Editor: Laura Scott
Associate Editor: June Sprunger
Copy Editor: Cathy Reef
Graphs/Drawings: Miriam Zacharias, Jessica Rothe, Allison Rothe

Photography: Tammy Christian, Jeff Chilcote, Tammy Cromer-Campbell, Nancy Sharp, Vicki Macy
Photography Assistants: Linda Quinlan, Arlou Witwer

Production Coordinator: Brenda Gallmeyer
Creative Coordinator: Shaun Venish
Book Design/Production: Dan Kraner
Traffic Coordinator: Sandra Beres

Publishers: Carl H. Muselman, Arthur K. Muselman
Chief Executive Officer: John Robinson
Marketing Director: Scott Moss
Editorial Director: Vivian Rothe
Production Director: George Hague

Printed in the United States of America
First Printing: 1999
Library of Congress Number: 98-73375
ISBN: 1-882138-41-4

Every effort has been made to ensure the accuracy and completeness of the instructions in this book. However, we cannot be responsible for human error or for the results when using materials other than those specified in the instructions, or for variations in individual work.

A Warm Welcome

Since becoming a plastic canvas book and magazine editor in 1992, I've been amazed over and over again at the generosity of plastic canvas hobbyists. It is a fact that most of you give away the majority of the projects you so carefully stitch. You give them as birthday and Christmas gifts, wedding and baby shower gifts, and "just because."

While in the planning stages of this book, my staff tried to think of your most frequent gift-giving occasions, and who are the lucky recipients of your projects. With these thoughts in mind, we divided this book into 10 full chapters. In each chapter, you'll find a collection of specialty gifts that we hope meet your every gift-giving occasion.

When you're short on time, "Last-Minute Gifts" will give you a great gift idea you can stitch up in just a few hours. "Keepsake Gifts" includes projects that will take a little more time, but are sure to become treasured keepsakes your family and friends will cherish. If Father's Day or your husband's birthday is coming up, "Just for Him" will give you a selection of tasteful, masculine gift ideas, while "Just for Her" will help you in expressing your affection for your mother, sister or special female friend.

Our "Just for Kids" brings you bright and colorful gifts that are as fun to play with as they are cheery. "For Our Pet Pals" makes sure we don't forget to treat our furry and feathered friends to a special treat now and again.

If you have a housewarming party to plan for, "Welcome Home" has many decorative home accents sure to be used. "Celebrate Love" includes gifts perfect for celebrating a couple's engagement, wedding or anniversary.

"Baby Love" features an assortment of baby items and nursery accessories the new mom and dad will enjoy. Finally, "Gift Bags for All" brings you a number of attractive gift bags and boxes in which to tuck your hand-stitched gift, thus giving two wonderful gifts in one!

For all these special occasions and more, we hope this collection of 85 delightful gifts will bring you stitching pleasure and joy in sharing.

Warm regards,

Laura Scott

Editor
Plastic Canvas All-Occasion Gifts

Contents

Chapter 5: **Just for Her**

Chapter 6: **For Our Pet Pals**

Chapter 7: **Celebrate Love**

Chapter 8: **Welcome Home**

Chapter 9: **Baby Love**

Chapter 10: **Gift Bags for All**

Reference

Last-Minute Gifts

If you occasionally find yourself needing a quick gift for a party, shower or secret pal exchange, then this chapter will prove to be a great lifesaver and time-saver. From whimsical magnets to darling photo frames, each project in this collection of a dozen gifts can be stitched from start to finish in three hours or less!

Veggie Jar Tags

Designs by Vicki Blizzard

Share the bounty of your garden with friends, family and neighbors.
And, don't forget to label each gift with a colorful veggie tag!

Skill Level

Beginner

Materials

- ½ sheet Uniek Quick-Count 7-count plastic canvas
- Uniek Needloft plastic canvas yarn as listed in color key
- #16 tapestry needle
- 3 (6") lengths gold elastic cord
- Unruled index card
- Hot-glue gun

Instructions

1. Cut plastic canvas according to graphs.

2. Stitch pieces following graphs. Overcast tomato with red; Overcast corn and carrot with adjacent colors.

3. For carrot top, attach a 6" length of fern with a Lark's Head Knot (Fig. 1) where indicated on graph. Unravel ends. Work kernels on corn with yellow and straw French Knots. Using 1 ply mint, Straight Stitch leaves on tomato.

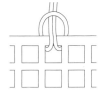

Fig. 1
Lark's Head Knot

4. Using red throughout, Overcast inside edges of tomato tag back and top edges of tomato tag front and back. Whipstitch wrong sides of tag front and back together around side and bottom edges.

5. Repeat step 4 for remaining two

tags, Overcasting and Whipstitching carrot tag with bittersweet and corn tag with yellow.

6. Center and glue carrot, corn and tomato to corresponding tag fronts.

7. Cut index card into three pieces that fit inside tags. Write jar contents on cards and place in tags.

8. For each tag, thread one length of elastic cord from tag back to tag front through holes indicated on graphs. Knot ends on tag front. Place tags over canning jars. ◆

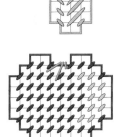

Corn
8 holes x 12 holes
Cut 1

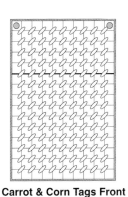

Carrot & Corn Tags Front
10 holes x 15 holes
Cut 2
Stitch 1 as graphed for carrot
Stitch 1 replacing bittersweet
with yellow for corn

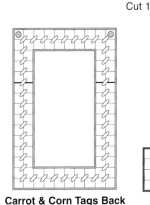

Carrot & Corn Tags Back
10 holes x 15 holes
Cut 2
Stitch 1 as graphed for carrot
Stitch 1 replacing bittersweet
with yellow for corn

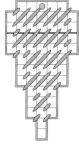

Tomato
10 holes x 8 holes
Cut 1

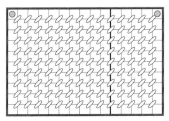

Tomato Tag Front
15 holes x 10 holes
Cut 1

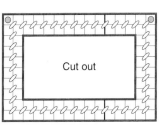

Cut out

Tomato Tag Back
15 holes x 10 holes
Cut 1

Carrot
7 holes x 13 holes
Cut 1

Tiny Treasures Music Box

Delight a loved one, young or old, with a special gift tucked inside this musical gift box. *Design by Vicki Blizzard*

Skill Level
Intermediate

Materials
- ½ sheet Uniek Quick-Count 7-count plastic canvas
- Uniek Needloft plastic canvas yarn as listed in color key
- Kreinik Medium (#16) Braid as listed in color key
- #16 tapestry needle
- 1¹¹⁄₁₆" x 1⅜" x ⁹⁄₁₆" 18-note miniature musical movement from Unicorn Studios
- 8½" x 12" sheet navy Charisma Luxury Suede from C.W. Fifield Co. Inc.
- 16 (3mm) crystal iris pearl beads from Darice
- 9 (6mm) crystal iris pearl beads from Darice
- Sewing needle and clear nylon thread
- Hot-glue gun (optional)

Cutting & Stitching
1. Cut plastic canvas according to graphs. Cut one 2½" square and one 6" circle from navy suede.

2. Stitch sides and top following graphs, working medium (#16) braid Backstitches over completed background stitching. Box bottom will remain unstitched.

3. With dark royal, Overcast around side and front edges of box top; Overcast top edges of three box sides.

4. Thread a length of medium (#16) braid from front to back through holes indicated on graph with red dots. Knot on back, forming a ¾" loop for box closure.

5. With sewing needle and clear thread attach one 3mm crystal iris bead in each hole indicated on box top. Attach 2½" square navy suede to wrong side of top with clear thread or hot glue.

6. With dark royal, Whipstitch sides together, then Whipstitch unstitched top edge of fourth box side to unstitched back edge of box top.

7. Using clear thread, attach one 6mm bead where indicated on graph to front side of box.

Final Assembly

1. Insert key on musical movement through opening on box bottom; center key in opening. Stitching through holes indicated on graph, wrap a 36" length of yarn around music box in two directions.

2. Using sewing needle and clear thread and following Fig. 1, bring needle down through one corner hole indicated for leg attachment on box bottom. Thread on one 6mm bead.

3. Thread needle through second 6mm bead, then back up through

Fig. 1

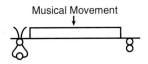

Musical Movement

top bead and out through second hole indicated in same corner. Tie thread securely, making sure beads are pulled tight against bottom.

4. Repeat steps 2 and 3 for remaining three legs.

5. With dark royal yarn, Whipstitch box bottom to box sides.

6. Using clear thread, sew a running stitch ⅛" from outside edge

of 6" suede circle. Gather circle enough so that opening of circle fits inside opening of box. Knot thread securely.

7. Place gathered circle inside box. Keeping open edge of circle even with top edges of sides, tuck suede down around musical movement. Using clear thread, sew suede lining in place. ◆

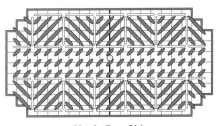

COLOR KEY	
Plastic Canvas Yarn	**Yards**
■ Dark royal #48	22
Medium (#16) Braid	
⁄ Pearl #032 Backstitch	7
⊙ Attach 3mm bead	
○ Attach 6mm bead	
✎ Attach musical movement	
● Attach leg	
Color numbers given are for Uniek Needloft plastic canvas yarn and Kreinik Medium (#16) Braid.	

Music Box Side
20 holes x 10 holes
Cut 4

Back Edge

Music Box Top
16 holes x 16 holes
Cut 1

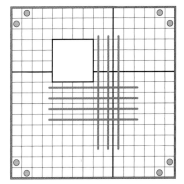

Music Box Bottom
16 holes x 16 holes
Cut 1
Do not stitch

Fancy Frames

Designs by Vicki Blizzard

Who doesn't like to display photos of their kids and grandkids?
Make it all the more enjoyable with these three colorful frames!

CHECKS & HEARTS

Skill Level

Beginner

Materials

- ◆ ½ sheet Uniek Quick-Count clear 7-count plastic canvas
- ◆ ½ sheet Uniek Quick-Count black 7-count plastic canvas
- ◆ Uniek Needloft plastic canvas yarn as listed in color key
- ◆ #16 tapestry needle
- ◆ 4 (4mm) ruby Austrian glass rhinestones #110-636-09 from National Artcraft
- ◆ Hot-glue gun

Instructions

1. Cut frame back and frame supports from black plastic canvas; cut flowers, hearts, leaves and frame front from clear plastic canvas according to graphs (right and page 12).

2. Stitch pieces following graphs, working Straight Stitches at center of leaves when background stitching is completed. Flowers, frame back and frame supports will remain unstitched.

3. Overcast hearts and leaves with adjacent colors. Overcast flowers with 1 ply yellow and inside opening of frame with 2 plies yellow.

4. With black, Whipstitch long straight edge of frame supports to frame back where indicated on frame back graph.

5. With Christmas red, Whipstitch frame front to frame back along outside edges.

6. Using photo as a guide, glue two leaves to each corner of photo opening. Center and glue one heart to top of each pair of leaves. Glue one flower to each frame corner. Glue one rhinestone to center of each flower.

Checks & Hearts Leaf
5 holes x 6 holes
Cut 8 from clear

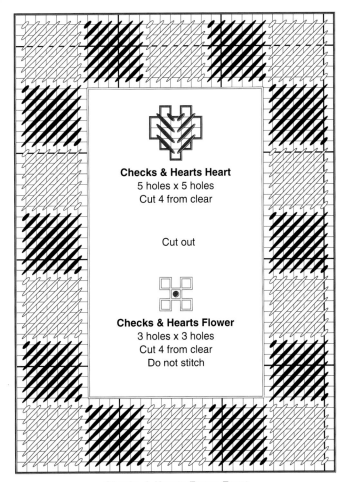

Checks & Hearts Heart
5 holes x 5 holes
Cut 4 from clear

Cut out

Checks & Hearts Flower
3 holes x 3 holes
Cut 4 from clear
Do not stitch

Checks & Hearts Frame Front
31 holes x 43 holes
Cut 1 from clear

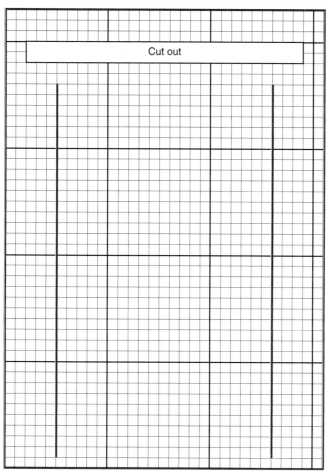

Cut out

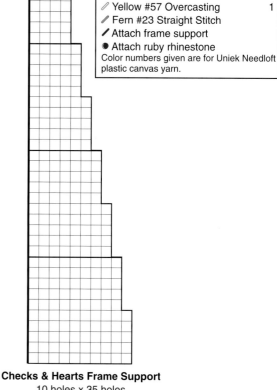

COLOR KEY
CHECKS & HEARTS

Plastic Canvas Yarn	Yards
■ Black #00	7
■ Christmas red #02	4
■ Fern #23	5
□ White #41	5
⁄ Yellow #57 Overcasting	1
⁄ Fern #23 Straight Stitch	
⁄ Attach frame support	
● Attach ruby rhinestone	

Color numbers given are for Uniek Needloft plastic canvas yarn.

Checks & Hearts Frame Back
31 holes x 43 holes
Cut 1 from black
Do not stitch

Checks & Hearts Frame Support
10 holes x 35 holes
Cut 2 from black
Do not stitch

BACHELOR BUTTONS

Skill Level
Beginner

Materials
◆ ¼ sheet Uniek Quick-Count clear 7-count plastic canvas
◆ ¼ sheet Uniek Quick-Count almond 7-count plastic canvas
◆ Uniek Needloft plastic canvas yarn as listed in color key
◆ #16 tapestry needle
◆ 15 small buttons in shades of rose, tan, red and blue
◆ Hot-glue gun

Instructions
1. Cut one frame back and one support from almond plastic canvas; cut frame front and leaves from clear plastic canvas according to graphs (right and page 13).

2. Stitch frame front and leaves following graphs, reversing four leaves before stitching. Work Straight Stitches at center of leaves when background stitching is completed. Frame back and frame support will remain unstitched.

3. Overcast leaves with holly. Using eggshell throughout, Overcast inside opening on frame front. Whipstitch long straight edge of frame support to frame back where indicated on frame back graph. Whipstitch frame front to frame back along outside edges.

4. Using photo as a guide, glue leaves to frame front. Glue assorted buttons as desired to frame front and to some leaves.

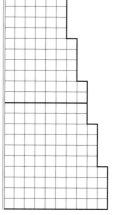

Bachelor Buttons Frame Support
10 holes x 20 holes
Cut 1 from almond
Do not stitch

Bachelor Buttons Leaf
5 holes x 6 holes
Cut 9, reverse 4, from clear

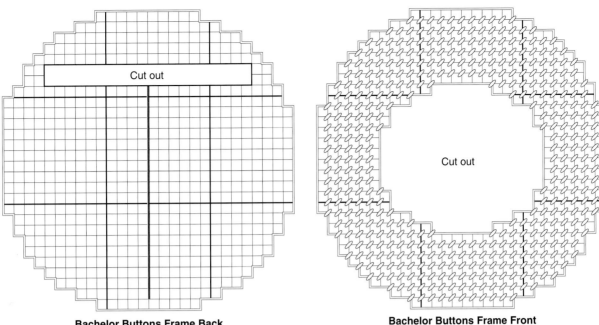

Bachelor Buttons Frame Back
28 holes x 28 holes
Cut 1 from almond
Do not stitch

Bachelor Buttons Frame Front
28 holes x 28 holes
Cut 1 from clear

SPARKLING STARS

Skill Level

Beginner

Materials List

◆ ¼ sheet Uniek Quick-Count clear 7-count plastic canvas

◆ ¼ sheet Uniek Quick-Count royal blue 7-count plastic canvas

◆ 4 plastic canvas star shapes by Uniek

◆ Uniek Needloft plastic canvas yarn as listed in color key

◆ ⅛"-wide Plastic Canvas 7 Metallic Needlepoint Yarn by Rainbow Gallery as listed in color key

◆ #16 tapestry needle

◆ 4 (6mm) round gold beads #705-125 by The Beadery

◆ Sewing needle and clear nylon thread

◆ Hot-glue gun

Instructions

1. Cut one frame back and two frame supports from royal blue plastic canvas; cut frame front and hearts from clear plastic

COLOR KEY
BACHELOR BUTTONS

Plastic Canvas Yarn	Yards
■ Holly #27	6
□ Eggshell #39	11
╱ Holly #27 Straight Stitch	
╱ Attach frame support	

Color numbers given are for Uniek Needloft plastic canvas yarn.

canvas (right and page 22).

2. Stitch hearts and frame front following graphs. Frame back and frame support will remain unstitched.

3. Overcast hearts with Christmas red. Using dark royal through step 4, Overcast inside opening of photo frame.

4. Whipstitch long straight edge of frame supports to frame back where indicated on frame back graph. Whipstitch frame front to frame back along outside edges.

5. Cut stars from plastic canvas star shapes following graph (page 22), cutting away shaded gray area on graph.

6. Stitch stars following graph. Overcast with gold.

7. Using sewing needle and clear thread, attach one gold bead to

center of each star where indicated on graph.

8. Using photo as a guide, glue stars to corners of frame front. Center hearts between stars on frame front and glue in place. ◆

Sparkling Stars Heart
5 holes x 5 holes
Cut 4 from clear

COLOR KEY
SPARKLING STARS

Plastic Canvas Yarn	Yards
■ Christmas red #02	2
■ Dark royal #48	14
⅛" Metallic Needlepoint Yarn	
□ White pearl #PC10	4
╱ Gold #PC1 Overcasting	2
○ Attach gold bead	
╱ Attach frame support	

Color numbers given are for Uniek Needloft plastic canvas yarn and Rainbow Gallery Plastic Canvas 7 Metallic Needlepoint Yarn.

Graphs continued on page 22

Whether you give these character magnets to teenagers or fun-loving friends, they're sure to appreciate your cool sense of humor!

Designs by Vicki Blizzard

BLACK SHEEP

Skill Level
Beginner

Materials
- ½ sheet Uniek Quick-Count 7-count plastic canvas
- Red Heart Classic worsted weight yarn Art. E267 as listed in color key
- Anchor #3 pearl cotton as listed in color key
- Kreinik Medium (#16) Braid as listed in color key
- #16 tapestry needle
- Small amount black mini-curl doll hair from One & Only Creations
- 2 (6mm) round black cabochons from The Beadery
- 3" square bandanna-print fabric
- Scrap white felt
- 6" ½"-wide magnet strip
- 7 (7mm) gold jump rings
- Needle-nose pliers
- Hot-glue gun

Instructions
1. Cut plastic canvas according to graphs (page 16).

2. Stitch pieces following graphs. Overcast all pieces with black. Work Backstitches on muzzle with pearl cotton and on sign with medium (#16) braid when

stitching and Overcasting are completed.

3. Glue ears, muzzle and cabochons for eyes to head following Fig. 1. For kerchief, cut bandanna fabric square diagonally in half, forming a triangle.

4. Using photo as a guide through step 7, glue kerchief ends behind head, placing point of triangle slightly off center. Center and glue head to body.

5. Cut black mini-curl doll hair in ½" lengths. Glue curls to body around head and bandanna.

6. Cut magnet strip into two 3" lengths; glue each length to back of body. Cut felt slightly smaller than sign and glue to backside.

7. With needle-nose pliers, attach one jump ring to each hole indicated on sign and body. Join body and sign rings with a third jump ring, as in photo, on each side. Attach remaining jump ring to one ear where indicated on graph.

COOL BEANS

Skill Level

Beginner

Materials

◆ ¼ sheet Uniek Quick-Count clear 7-count plastic canvas

◆ Small amount black 7-count plastic canvas

◆ Red Heart Classic worsted weight yarn Art. E267 as listed in color key

◆ ⅛"-wide Plastic Canvas 7 Metallic Needlepoint Yarn by Rainbow Gallery as listed in color key

◆ Anchor #3 pearl cotton as listed in color key

◆ #16 tapestry needle

◆ 4" ½"-wide magnet strip

◆ Scrap white felt

◆ 6 (7mm) silver jump rings

◆ Needle-nose pliers

◆ Hot-glue gun

Instructions

1. Cut one sign and two beans from clear plastic canvas; cut two sunglasses from black plastic canvas according to graphs.

2. Stitch pieces following graphs, reversing one bean before stitching. When background stitching is completed, work French Knots and Straight Stitches on sign with 2 plies country red; Backstitch mouths on beans with pearl cotton.

3. Overcast sunglasses where indicated on graph with black; do not Overcast bridges. Overcast beans with country red and sign with true blue and country red, alternating colors.

4. Cut felt slightly smaller than sign and glue to backside. Cut magnet strip into two 2" lengths; glue strips to backside of sign along side edges.

5. Using photo as a guide through step 6, glue sunglasses to beans.

6. With needle-nose pliers, attach one jump ring to each bean where indicated on graph. Attach one jump ring to each hole on sign where indicated on graph. Join each bean to sign with a third jump ring. ◆

COLOR KEY
COOL BEANS

Worsted Weight Yarn	Yards
■ True blue #822	3
■ Country red #914	9
Uncoded area on sign is white	
#1 Continental Stitches	5
╱ Black #12 Overcasting	1
╱ Country red #914 Straight Stitch	
● Country red #914 French Knot	
#3 Pearl Cotton	
╱ Medium coral #9 Backstitch	¼
⅛" Metallic Needlepoint	
▢ Silver #PC2	1
○ Attach jump ring	

Color numbers given are for Red Heart Classic worsted weight yarn Art. E267, Anchor #3 pearl cotton and Rainbow Gallery Plastic Canvas 7 Metallic Needlepoint Yarn.

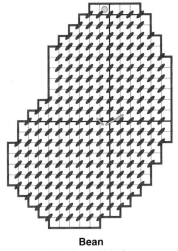

Bean
16 holes x 21 holes
Cut 2, reverse 1, from clear

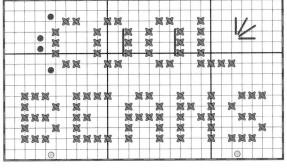

Cool Bean Sign
27 holes x 15 holes
Cut 1 from clear

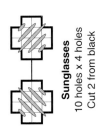

Sunglasses
10 holes x 4 holes
Cut 2 from black

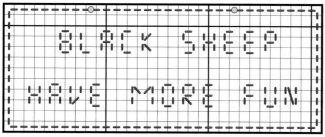

Black Sheep Sign
31 holes x 12 holes
Cut 1

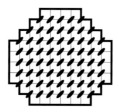

Black Sheep Head
10 holes x 9 holes
Cut 1

Black Sheep Ear
5 holes x 3 holes
Cut 2

Fig. 1

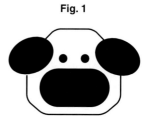

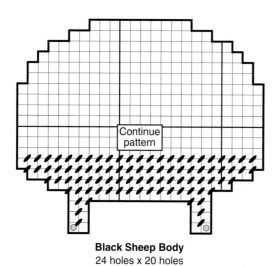

Continue pattern

Black Sheep Body
24 holes x 20 holes
Cut 1

Black Sheep Muzzle
7 holes x 4 holes
Cut 1

Delightful Daisy
Musical Magnet

Design by Vicki Blizzard

The title of this whimsical project says it all! Stitch it for a friend today as a cheery pick-me-up gift!

Skill Level

Beginner

Materials

- ¼ sheet Uniek Quick-Count 7-count plastic canvas
- 2 (3") plastic canvas radial circles
- Uniek Needloft plastic canvas yarn as listed in color key
- DMC #3 pearl cotton as listed in color key
- #16 tapestry needle
- 4mm ruby round faceted bead from The Beadery
- 2 (10mm) oval movable eyes
- Electronic music button in desired tune from National Artcraft
- 1" round magnet button
- Ceramic ladybug button #86050 by Mill Hill Products from Gay Bowles Sales, Inc.
- 12" ⅜"-wide red dotted swiss grosgrain ribbon
- Hot-glue gun

Instructions

1. Cut petals, cheeks and head side from 7-count plastic canvas according to graphs.

2. Stitch pieces following graphs, Overlapping one hole on head side before stitching. Overcast cheeks and petals with adjacent colors, Whipstitching bottom dart of each petal together as indicated while Overcasting.

3. Cut off four outside rows of holes from both radial circles following graph.

4. Stitch each circle following graph. With Christmas red pearl cotton, Backstitch mouth and attach bead for nose where indicated on graph on head front only.

5. Whipstitch head front and head back to head side. Before closing completely, insert musical button inside circle, with silver circle on button facing head front.

6. Using photo as a guide through step 8, glue eyes and cheeks to head front.

7. Spacing evenly around face, glue large petals between the two rows of stitching on head side. Glue small petals around face to head side, placing them in front of and between large petals.

8. Tie red ⅜"-wide ribbon in a bow; trim ends at an angle. Glue bow just below face on lower right side. Glue ladybug to a large petal on left side. Glue magnet on back. ◆

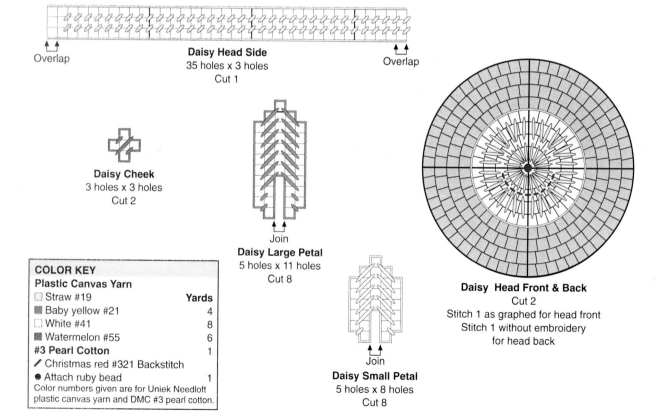

Daisy Head Side
35 holes x 3 holes
Cut 1

Overlap   Overlap

Daisy Cheek
3 holes x 3 holes
Cut 2

Join
Daisy Large Petal
5 holes x 11 holes
Cut 8

Daisy Head Front & Back
Cut 2
Stitch 1 as graphed for head front
Stitch 1 without embroidery
for head back

Join
Daisy Small Petal
5 holes x 8 holes
Cut 8

COLOR KEY	
Plastic Canvas Yarn	
☐ Straw #19	**Yards**
■ Baby yellow #21	4
☐ White #41	8
■ Watermelon #55	6
#3 Pearl Cotton	1
✓ Christmas red #321 Backstitch	
● Attach ruby bead	1
Color numbers given are for Uniek Needloft plastic canvas yarn and DMC #3 pearl cotton.	

Singing
Birdhouse Magnet

Design by Vicki Blizzard

Tuck a motion detector inside this pretty magnet to surprise your guests.
Every time someone walks past this songbird, she'll sing!

Skill Level

Beginner

Materials

- ½ sheet Uniek Quick-Count 7-count plastic canvas
- Red Heart Classic worsted weight yarn Art. E267 as listed in color key
- #16 tapestry needle
- 20 (6mm) translucent petal-pink baby's breath flower beads #880-190 from The Beadery
- 20 light yellow glass seed beads #02002 by Mill Hill Products from Gay Bowles Sales, Inc.
- Motion-activated chirping-bird sound device #214-919-00 from National Artcraft
- Beading needle and clear thread
- ⅝" mauve mushroom bird
- 6" ½"-wide magnet strip
- Hot-glue gun

Instructions

1. Cut plastic canvas according to graphs, cutting out sound-device hole at top on birdhouse front only.

2. Stitch pieces following graphs, stitching birdhouse back with country blue Slanting Gobelin Stitches only. Perch will remain unstitched.

3. Overcast fence, eaves and perch with white.

4. Using country blue through step 5, Whipstitch short edges of birdhouse pieces together as follows: side to roof, roof to roof, roof to side, side to bottom, and bottom to remaining short edge of first side.

5. Whipstitch back to roof, sides and bottom. Insert sound-device box into birdhouse, tucking excess wire around box. Insert tip of sensor into opening on birdhouse front. Whipstitch front to roof, sides and bottom.

6. Using photo as a guide through step 7, with clear thread and beading needle, sew flowers to fence and eaves, attaching seed beads to center of flowers at the same time.

7. Glue eaves to front along roof edge. Glue fence to front, making sure bottom edges are even. Glue short edge of perch to front where indicated on graph. Glue bird to perch.

8. Cut magnet strip into three equal pieces and glue to back of birdhouse. ◆

COLOR KEY	
Worsted Weight Yarn	**Yards**
□ White #1	3
■ Black #12	1
▨ Country blue #882	9
○ Attach perch	
Color numbers given are for Red Heart Classic worsted weight yarn Art. E267.	

Birdhouse Roof
5 holes x 9 holes
Cut 2

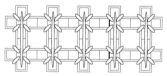

Birdhouse Fence
15 holes x 6 holes
Cut 1

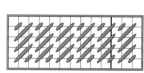

Birdhouse Bottom
13 holes x 5 holes
Cut 1

Birdhouse Perch
1 hole x 5 holes
Cut 1
Do not stitch

Cut out for front only

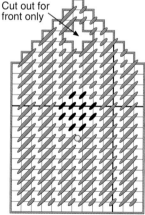

Birdhouse Front & Back
13 holes x 20 holes
Cut 2
Stitch front as graphed
Stitch back with country blue pattern only

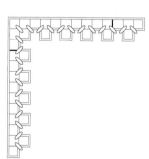

Birdhouse Eaves
13 holes x 13 holes
Cut 1

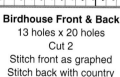

Birdhouse Side
5 holes x 14 holes
Cut 2

Busy Bee
Bookmark

Design by Vicki Blizzard

Give this colorful bookmark along with
a new best seller to a book-loving friend!

Skill Level
Beginner

Materials
◆ ¼ sheet Uniek Quick-Count 7-count plastic canvas
◆ Red Heart Classic worsted weight yarn Art. E267 as listed in color key
◆ ⅛"-wide Plastic Canvas 7 Metallic Needlepoint Yarn by Rainbow Gallery as listed in color key
◆ #16 tapestry needle
◆ 12" ⅞"-wide ribbon in desired color
◆ Fray preventative
◆ Hot-glue gun

Instructions
1. Cut plastic canvas according to graphs.

2. Stitch pieces following graphs, working Straight Stitches on leaves when background stitching is completed. Overcast edges following graphs.

3. Apply fray preventative to both ends of ribbon. Allow to dry.

4. Glue wings to bee front where indicated with blue lines. Glue bee to backside of ribbon at one end.

5. Glue leaves to back of flower at three sides. Glue assembled flower to right side of ribbon at remaining end. ◆

COLOR KEY

Worsted Weight Yarn	Yards
■ Black #12	1
□ Yellow #230	1
▨ Paddy green #686	3
▨ Grenadine #730	1
╱ Paddy green #686 Straight Stitch	
⅛" Metallic Needlepoint Yarn	
□ White pearl #PC10	2

Color numbers given are for Red Heart Classic worsted weight yarn Art. E267 and Rainbow Gallery Plastic Canvas 7 Metallic Needlepoint Yarn.

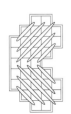

Bookmark Bee Wing
5 holes x 9 holes
Cut 2

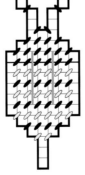

Bookmark Bee
7 holes x 16 holes
Cut 1

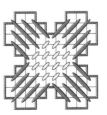

Bookmark Flower
9 holes x 9 holes
Cut 1

Bookmark Leaf
7 holes x 9 holes
Cut 3

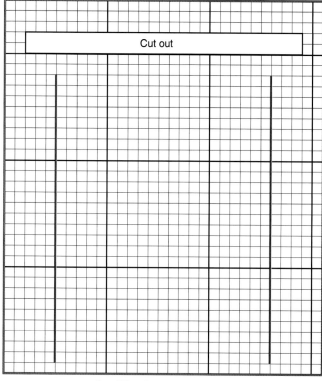

Sparkling Stars Frame Back
31 holes x 35 holes
Cut 1 from royal blue
Do not stitch

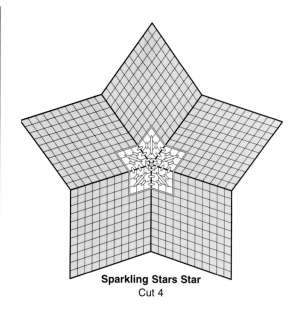

Sparkling Stars Star
Cut 4

COLOR KEY	
SPARKLING STARS	
Plastic Canvas Yarn	**Yards**
■ Christmas red #02	2
■ Dark royal #48	14
⅛" Metallic Needlepoint Yarn	
☐ White pearl #PC10	4
⁄ Gold #PC1 Overcasting	2
◉ Attach gold bead	
⁄ Attach frame support	
Color numbers given are for Uniek Needloft plastic canvas yarn and Rainbow Gallery Plastic Canvas 7 Metallic Needlepoint Yarn.	

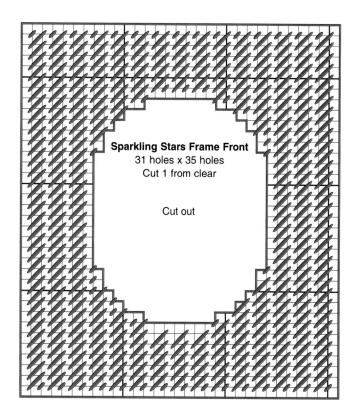

Sparkling Stars Frame Front
31 holes x 35 holes
Cut 1 from clear

Cut out

Sparkling Stars Frame Support
10 holes x 27 holes
Cut 2 from royal blue
Do not stitch

Keepsake Gifts

Every now and again we want to give a special, hand-stitched gift that will touch the heart of the recipient. This collection of keepsake gifts, from jewel boxes to photograph frames, will express your affection with style and warmth.

Angelic Music Box

Design by Vicki Blizzard

This enchanting music box makes a memorable gift. Three darling guardian angels will add a heavenly touch to the home.

Skill Level

Advanced

Materials

- ◆ *2 sheets 7-count regular plastic canvas*
- ◆ *Lengthwise ¼ artist-size sheet 7-count soft plastic canvas*
- ◆ *2 (4½") plastic canvas radial circles from Darice*
- ◆ *Uniek Needloft plastic canvas yarn as listed in color key*
- ◆ *Uniek Needloft metallic craft cord as listed in color key*
- ◆ *#3 pearl cotton as listed in color key*
- ◆ *#16 tapestry needle*
- ◆ *1 yard ⅛"-wide white satin ribbon*
- ◆ *24" ⅞"-wide white beaded lace ruffle*
- ◆ *6 (5mm) black round cabochons from The Beadery*
- ◆ *1⅛" mushroom mini fat chickadee #1615-51 from Darice*
- ◆ *Winter white mini-curl doll hair from One & Only Creations*
- ◆ *18-note musical movement from National Artcraft*
- ◆ *Music box adhesive mounting pad from National Artcraft*
- ◆ *4" clear plastic music box turntable from National Artcraft*
- ◆ *Polyester fiberfill*
- ◆ *Hot-glue gun*

Cutting

1. Cut five clouds, six angel bodies, 12 angel arms, three halos, six each of wings A and B, two crosses and two hearts from regular plastic canvas following graphs (page 25).

2. Cut one box side from soft plastic canvas according to graph (page 25). Cut one 9-hole x 55-hole piece from soft plastic canvas for music movement support. Support will remain unstitched.

3. Cut away crossbars in the shaded gray area at center of one plastic canvas circle for box bottom (page 28). Do not cut remaining circle, which is the box top.

4. Cut both lace ruffle and ribbon into three equal lengths.

Music Box

1. Stitch clouds and side following graphs, overlapping one hole on side before stitching. Overcast clouds with white and solid silver following graph.

2. Using bright blue through step 6, Overcast center opening on box bottom. Stitch bottom from center out following graph. When last row is completed, without cutting yarn, Whipstitch bottom to box side, beginning at overlapped seam.

3. Roll support into a cylinder, overlapping one hole; Whipstitch together. Remove music movement key. Apply adhesive pad to bottom of music movement.

4. Remove paper from other side of pad; line up hole in bottom of music movement with opening on box bottom. Press music movement firmly into place. Apply a thick line of hot glue around outside edge of music movement, then place unstitched support around movement in glue.

5. Stitch box top from center out following graph. Without cutting yarn, Whipstitch top to side, beginning at overlapped seam.

6. Glue clouds evenly spaced around box side. Insert turntable into music box through center opening on box bottom.

Angels

1. Following graphs throughout, stitch and Overcast halos with solid gold. Stitch remaining pieces, working uncoded areas with baby pink Continental Stitches. Work heads on body backs with baby pink Continental Stitches only; reverse six arms before stitching. Work pearl cotton Straight Stitches on angel faces.

2. Overcast bottom edges of angel bodies with white. For each angel, Whipstitch wrong sides of one front and one back together along sides and top following graph, stuffing head with fiberfill before closing. Firmly stuff bodies from bottom opening.

3. Thread one length of ribbon through needle, then weave through beaded edge of one ruffle. Pull ribbon to gather; make

ribbon ends even. Repeat with remaining ribbons and ruffles.

4. Using photo as a guide through step 9, tie one ribbon in a bow around neck of each angel, leaving ends trailing. Evenly distribute gathers of ruffle around neck. Trim ribbon ends at an angle.

5. Whipstitch wrong sides of one wing A and one wing B together with white. Repeat with remaining wing pieces. Glue one pair of wings to back of each angel.

6. Matching edges, Whipstitch wrong sides of two arms together with adjacent colors. Repeat with remaining arm pieces. With thumbs facing up, glue top of one arm to each shoulder.

7. Following manufacturer's directions, glue hair to backs of heads and around faces; trim as desired. Glue one halo to head of each angel. For eyes, glue two black cabochons to each face directly under eyebrows.

8. Whipstitch wrong sides of crosses together with solid gold. Whipstitch wrong sides of hearts together with pink.

9. Glue angels evenly spaced around top of base. Glue mushroom bird in hands of one angel, cross in hands of another angel and heart in hands of remaining angel. ◆

COLOR KEY

Plastic Canvas Yarn	Yards
■ Pink #07	4
□ White #41	66
■ Bright blue #60	44
Uncoded areas are baby pink #08 Continental Stitches	17
⁄ Baby pink #08 Whipstitching	
Metallic Craft Cord	
■ Solid gold #20	4
■ Solid silver #21	2
#3 Pearl Cotton	
⁄ White Straight Stitch	1
Color numbers given are for Uniek Needloft plastic canvas yarn and Needloft Craft Cord.	

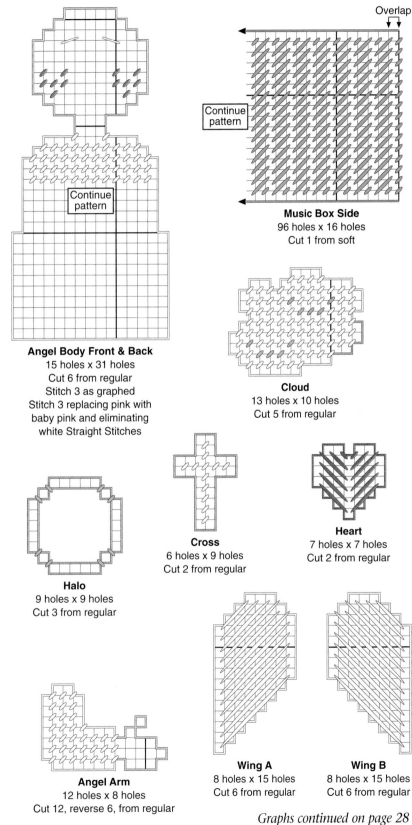

Continue pattern

Angel Body Front & Back
15 holes x 31 holes
Cut 6 from regular
Stitch 3 as graphed
Stitch 3 replacing pink with baby pink and eliminating white Straight Stitches

Overlap

Continue pattern

Music Box Side
96 holes x 16 holes
Cut 1 from soft

Cloud
13 holes x 10 holes
Cut 5 from regular

Halo
9 holes x 9 holes
Cut 3 from regular

Cross
6 holes x 9 holes
Cut 2 from regular

Heart
7 holes x 7 holes
Cut 2 from regular

Angel Arm
12 holes x 8 holes
Cut 12, reverse 6, from regular

Wing A
8 holes x 15 holes
Cut 6 from regular

Wing B
8 holes x 15 holes
Cut 6 from regular

Graphs continued on page 28

Triple Photo Frame

Design by Vicki Blizzard

This handsome and decorative frame makes a lovely photo display for any room in your home.

Skill Level

Intermediate

Materials

- 4 sheets Uniek Quick-Count 7-count plastic canvas
- Uniek Needloft plastic canvas yarn as listed in color key
- Kreinik Medium (#16) Braid as listed in color key
- #16 tapestry needle
- 2" wooden ball
- Delta Ceramcoat straw #2078 acrylic paint
- Delta Renaissance Foil Easy Gold Leafing System antique gold kit

port from plastic canvas according to graphs (below and page 28).

3. Stitch frame fronts and backs following graphs. Stitch support with stitches shown on graph, leaving bars with blue lines unstitched; do not overlap at this time.

4. Overcast inside edges of frame fronts and backs with burgundy. Work Backstitches on frame fronts with gold braid.

5. Using burgundy through step 7, Whipstitch wrong sides of one frame front and one frame back together around bottom, right side and top edges, leaving edges on left side between blue dots

unstitched. Repeat for remaining two frames.

6. Whipstitch left side of one frame between blue dots to one unstitched bar on support, stitching through all three thicknesses. Repeat with remaining frames and unstitched bars.

7. Roll support into a cylinder, overlapping where indicated and placing left edge on top; stitch together with Continental Stitches. Overcast top and bottom edges.

8. Apply a thick line of hot glue to inside top edge of support. Insert gold ball into top of support; hold in place until set. ◆

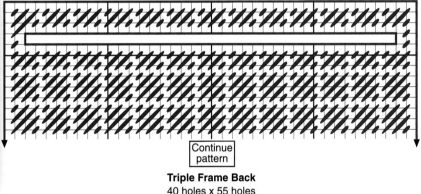

Triple Frame Back
40 holes x 55 holes
Cut 3

Overlap   Overlap

Triple Frame Support
42 holes x 61 holes
Cut 1

◆ Paintbrush

◆ Hot-glue gun

Instructions

1. Paint wooden ball with two coats straw acrylic paint. Allow to dry thoroughly. Following manufacturer's directions for gold leafing system, apply one coat sealer and two coats adhesive to painted ball. Apply foil, making sure all spots are covered and ball is no longer sticky. Set aside.

2. Cut three frame fronts, three frame backs and one frame sup-

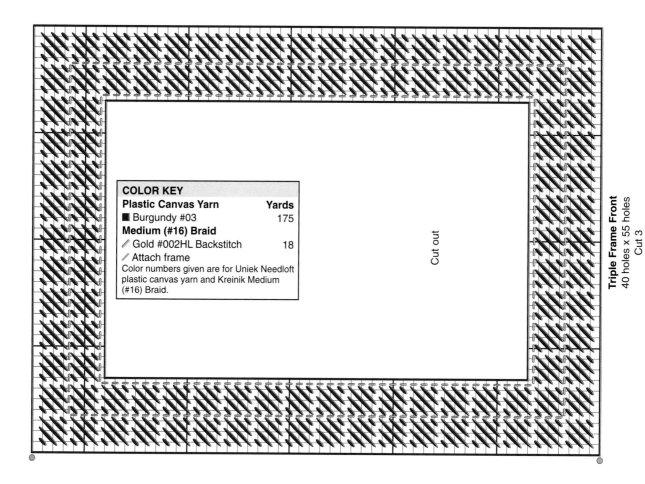

COLOR KEY

Plastic Canvas Yarn	Yards
■ Burgundy #03	175
Medium (#16) Braid	
⟋ Gold #002HL Backstitch	18
⟋ Attach frame	

Color numbers given are for Uniek Needloft plastic canvas yarn and Kreinik Medium (#16) Braid.

Cut out

Triple Frame Front
40 holes x 55 holes
Cut 3

ANGELIC MUSIC BOX

Continued from page 25

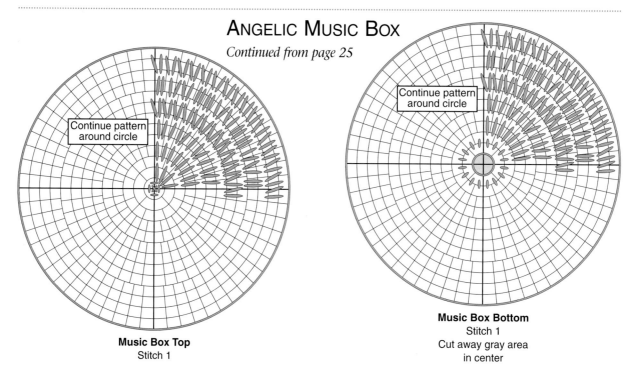

Continue pattern around circle

Continue pattern around circle

Music Box Top
Stitch 1

Music Box Bottom
Stitch 1
Cut away gray area
in center

Bargello Jewel Box

Design by Joan Green

Rich colors and golden accents make this attractive jewelry box extra-special.

Skill Level

Intermediate

Materials

◆ 2 sheets Darice Ultra Stiff 7-count plastic canvas

◆ Spinrite Bernat Berella "4" worsted weight yarn as listed in color key

◆ 1/16"-wide Plastic Canvas 10 Metallic Needlepoint Yarn by Rainbow Gallery as listed in color key

◆ #16 tapestry needle

◆ 7mm round faceted stones from The Beadery:
8 turquoise #026
4 dark fuchsia #085

◆ Thick white craft glue

◆ 7" x 5⅛" piece tan self-adhesive felt (optional)

Project Note

Use 6 plies yarn for stitching bargello design. Use 4 plies for all other worsted weight yarn stitching.

Instructions

1. Cut box sides, lid sides and lid top from stiff plastic canvas according to graphs. Cut one 47-hole x 35-hole piece for box bottom.

2. For tray, cut one 45-hole x 33-hole piece for bottom, two 45-hole x 8-hole pieces for long sides, three 33-hole x 8-hole pieces for short sides and middle divider, one 23-hole x 8-hole piece for large section divider and one 22-hole x 8 hole piece for small section divider.

3. Box bottom and tray pieces will remain unstitched. Stitch remaining pieces following graphs and Project Note, working uncoded areas with medium teal Continental Stitches.

4. Work gold Straight Stitches and French Knots over completed background stitching.

5. Using medium damson throughout, Overcast bottom edges of lid sides. Whipstitch sides together, then Whipstitch sides to lid top.

6. Using medium teal throughout, Overcast top edges of box sides. Whipstitch sides together, then Whipstitch sides to box bottom.

7. For tray, using pale teal and assembly diagram through step 8, Whipstitch two long sides to two short sides, then Whipstitch sides to bottom.

8. Whipstitch middle divider to 22nd bar of both long sides. Whipstitch small section divider slightly off center in the 22-hole x 33-hole section. Whipstitch large section divider slightly off center in the 23-hole x 33-hole section.

9. Glue faceted stones to lid top where indicated on graph. If desired, attach felt to bottom side of box bottom. Place tray inside box. ◆

COLOR KEY	
Worsted Weight Yarn	**Yards**
▨ Pale teal #8844	50
▨ Pale damson #8853	7
■ Medium damson #8855	15
Uncoded areas are medium teal #8844 Continental Stitches	22
╱ Medium teal #8844 Overcasting and Whipstitching	
1/16" Metallic Needlepoint Yarn	
╱ Gold #PM51 Straight Stitch	8
○ Gold #PM51 French Knot	
● Attach turquoise stone	
● Attach dark fuchsia stone	
Color numbers given are for Spinrite Bernat Berella "4" worsted weight yarn and Rainbow Gallery Plastic Canvas 10 Metallic Needlepoint Yarn.	

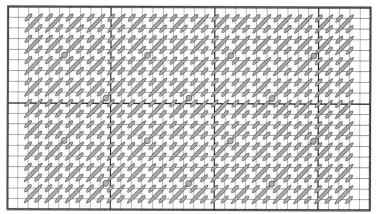

Jewel Box Short Sides
35 holes x 19 holes
Cut 2

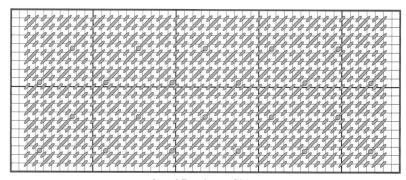

Jewel Box Long Sides
47 holes x 19 holes
Cut 2

Jewel Box Lid Long Side
49 holes x 3 holes
Cut 2

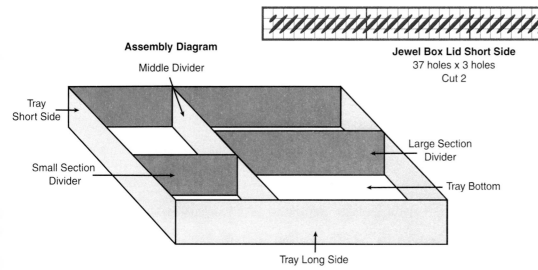

Assembly Diagram

Middle Divider

Tray
Short Side

Small Section
Divider

Jewel Box Lid Short Side
37 holes x 3 holes
Cut 2

Large Section
Divider

Tray Bottom

Tray Long Side

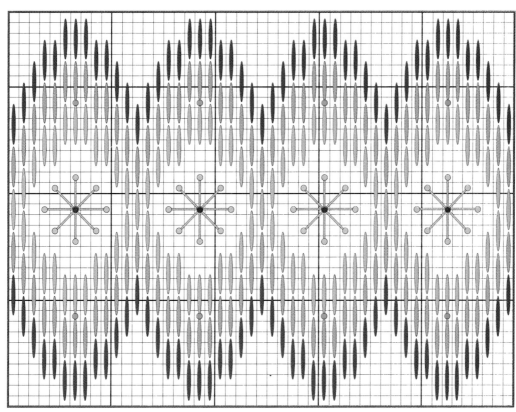

Jewel Box Lid Top
49 holes x 37 holes
Cut 1

Pastel **Treasures**

Designs by Lilo Fruehwirth

Whether given to a couple or a friend who enjoys feminine items, this frame and trinket box set makes a cherished gift.

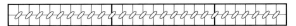

Pastel Treasures Streamer
27 holes x 2 holes
Cut 2

COLOR KEY	
6-Strand Embroidery Floss	**Yards**
☐ White	157

Pastel Treasures Bow
43 holes x 2 holes
Cut 2

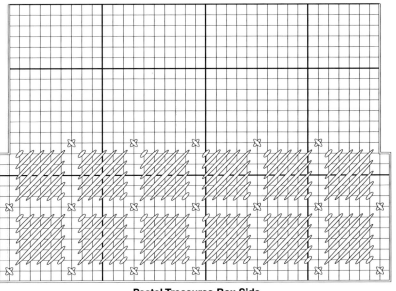

Pastel Treasures Box Side
38 holes x 26 holes
Cut 4

Skill Level

Beginner

Materials

- ◆ *2 sheets pink 10-count plastic canvas*
- ◆ *6-strand embroidery floss as listed in color key*
- ◆ *#18 tapestry needle*
- ◆ *2 (18") lengths 4mm white string pearls*
- ◆ *2 small white satin roses*
- ◆ *Tacky craft glue*

Cutting & Stitching

1. Cut plastic canvas according to graphs, cutting out photo opening on frame front only. Cut two 19-hole x 57-hole pieces for easel and one 38-hole x 38-hole piece for box bottom.

2. Frame back, easel pieces and box bottom will remain unstitched. Using 12 strands floss through step 6, stitch remaining pieces following graphs.

3. Overcast top and inside edges of frame front, top edge of frame back and bottom edge of lid sides.

4. Whipstitch easel pieces together along side and bottom edges. Center easel on frame back, making sure bottom edges are even, then Whipstitch top edge of easel to frame back.

5. Whipstitch frame front and back together around side and bottom edges.

6. Whipstitch lid sides together, then Whipstitch lid sides to lid top. Whipstitch box sides together, then Whipstitch box sides to box bottom. Top edges of box sides are not Overcast.

Bow & Streamer

1. With 6 strands floss, Whipstitch short edges of one bow together, forming a ring.

Repeat with second bow.

2. Using photo as a guide through step 4, with seam at center back, form one ring into a bow by stitching through both layers of plastic canvas at bow center to middle of one streamer. Repeat with remaining bow and streamer.

3. Glue one bow and streamer to center of lid top. Glue remaining bow and streamer to upper left corner of frame front near photo opening.

4. Cut and shape one length of string pearls into loops and streamers; glue around bow on lid box as desired. Repeat with remaining length of string pearls and bow on frame. Glue one satin rose to top center of each bow. ◆

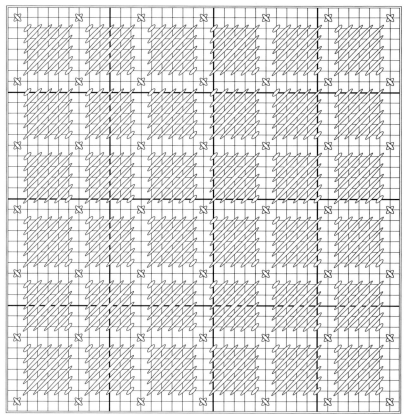

Pastel Treasures Box Lid Top
38 holes x 38 holes
Cut 1

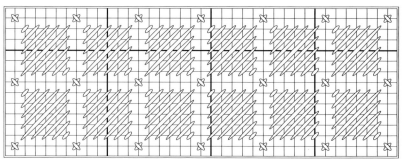

Pastel Treasures Box Lid Side
38 holes x 14 holes
Cut 4

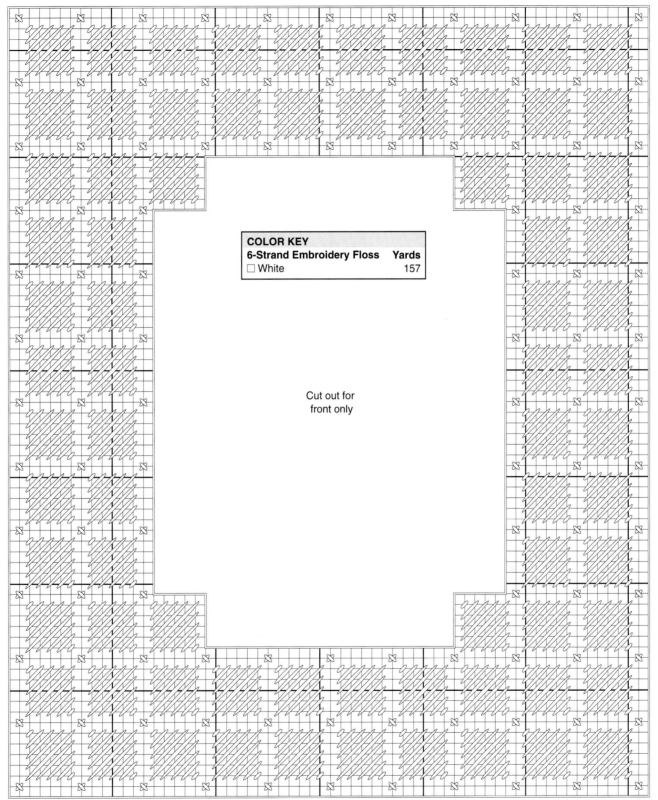

COLOR KEY

6-Strand Embroidery Floss	Yards
☐ White	157

Cut out for
front only

Pastel Treasures Frame Front & Back
62 holes x 74 holes
Cut 2
Stitch front as graphed
Do not stitch back

Embossed Flowers
Ensemble

Designs by Carol Nartowicz

Worked in colors to coordinate with a bedroom or bathroom,
this lovely set includes a tissue box cover and keepsake box.

Advanced

TISSUE BOX COVER

Materials

- 3 sheets 7-count plastic canvas
- Uniek Needloft plastic canvas yarn as listed in color key
- #16 tapestry needle
- Hot-glue gun

Instructions

1. Cut plastic canvas according to graphs (pages 38 and 39), cutting 68 flowers for cover panels.

2. Stitch pieces following graphs, leaving bars with blue lines and middle section of sides unstitched. Work Lazy Daisy Stitches on panels when background stitching is completed.

3. Overcast flowers with pink. Using lavender through step 6, Overcast inside edges of top and bottom edges of sides.

4. Whipstitch one top facing and one bottom facing to two side facings along short edges. Repeat with remaining facing pieces. Whipstitch one assembled facing to each panel.

5. Whipstitch facing on one panel to one side where indicated on graph with blue lines. Repeat with remaining side and panel pieces.

6. Whipstitch sides together, then Whipstitch sides to top.

7. Using photo as a guide, glue flowers to panels in clusters of twos, threes and fours as indicated.

KEEPSAKE BOX

Materials

- 3 sheets 7-count plastic canvas
- Uniek Needloft plastic canvas yarn as listed in color key
- #16 tapestry needle
- Hot-glue gun

Instructions

1. Cut plastic canvas according to graphs (below and pages 38 and 39), cutting 20 flowers for box large panels. Cut one 34-hole x 28-hole piece for box bottom, two 32-hole x 3-hole pieces for lid long facings and two 26-hole x 3-hole pieces for lid short facings.

2. Box bottom and lid facings will remain unstitched. Stitch remaining pieces following graphs, leaving middle sections of box sides and bars with blue lines on lid top and box sides unstitched.

3. Work Lazy Daisy Stitches on large panels when background stitching is completed. Overcast flowers with pink.

4. Using lavender through step 9, Overcast lid top, long edges of handle and top edges of box sides.

5. For lid, Whipstitch long facings to short facings along short edges, then Whipstitch facings to top with Continental Stitches at blue lines on graph. Overcast bottom edges of facings. Whipstitch short edges of handle to top where indicated on graph.

6. For small panels, Whipstitch one top and one bottom facing to two side facings along short edges. Repeat with remaining small panel facing pieces. Whipstitch one assembled facing to each panel.

7. Whipstitch facing of one small panel to one box short side where indicated on graph with blue lines. Repeat with remaining short box side and small panel.

8. Repeat steps 6 and 7 for large panel facings, large panels and box long sides.

9. Whipstitch box sides together, then Whipstitch sides to bottom. Using photo as guide, glue flowers to large panels in clusters of twos and fours as indicated on graph. ◆

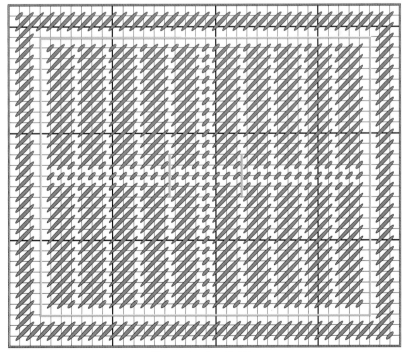

Keepsake Box Lid Top
38 holes x 32 holes
Cut 1

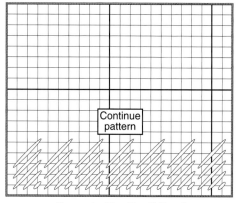

Keepsake Box Small Panel
22 holes x 18 holes
Cut 2

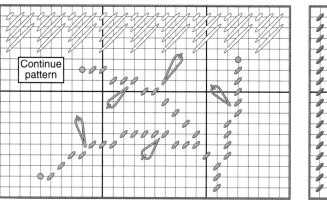

Keepsake Box Large Panel
28 holes x 18 holes
Cut 2

Keepsake Box Large Panel Side Facing
2 holes x 18 holes
Cut 4

Tissue Box Cover Top & Bottom Facing
25 holes x 2 holes
Cut 8

COLOR KEY	
KEEPSAKE BOX	
Plastic Canvas Yarn	**Yards**
■ Lavender #05	59
☐ Pink #07	2
■ Fern #23	3
☐ White #41	20
⬢ Fern #23 Lazy Daisy	
⦿ Attach 4 flowers	
⦿ Attach 2 flowers	
╱ Attach handle	
Color numbers given are for Uniek Needloft plastic canvas yarn.	

Ensemble Flower
3 holes x 3 holes
Cut 68 for tissue box cover
Cut 20 for keepsake box

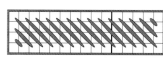

Keepsake Box Lid Handle
15 holes x 4 holes
Cut 1

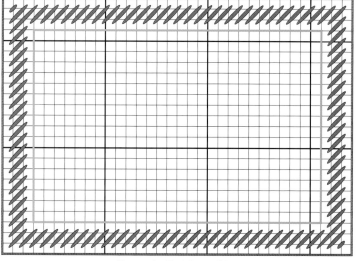

Keepsake Box Long Side
34 holes x 24 holes
Cut 2

Keepsake Box Small Panel Side Facing
2 holes x 18 holes
Cut 4

Tissue Box Cover Side Facing
2 holes x 31 holes
Cut 8

Keepsake Box Large Panel Top & Bottom Facing
28 holes x 2 holes
Cut 4

Keepsake Box Small Panel Top & Bottom Facing
22 holes x 2 holes
Cut 4

COLOR KEY
TISSUE BOX COVER

Plastic Canvas Yarn	Yards
■ Lavender #05	45
□ Pink #07	6
■ Fern #23	10
□ White #41	30

🖊 Fern #23 Lazy Daisy
● Attach 4 flowers
● Attach 3 flowers
● Attach 2 flowers
Color numbers given are for Uniek Needloft
plastic canvas yarn.

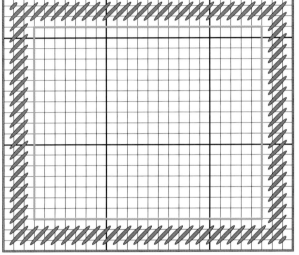

Keepsake Box Short Side
28 holes x 24 holes
Cut 2

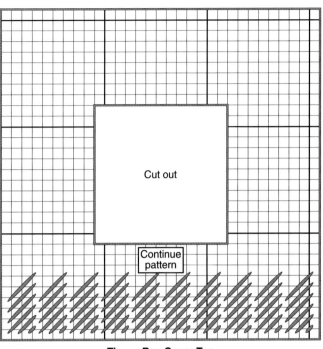

Tissue Box Cover Top
31 holes x 31 holes
Cut 1

Cut out

Continue pattern

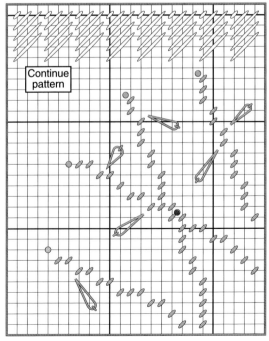

Continue pattern

Tissue Box Cover Panel
25 holes x 31 holes
Cut 4

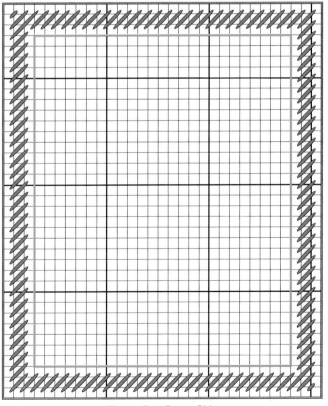

Tissue Box Cover Side
31 holes x 37 holes
Cut 4

Just for Kids

Delight your kids with this collection of fun and fanciful toys! Bright, cheery colors and innovative designs will make these toys among your children's favorites!

The Littlest Doghouse

Design by Louise Young

Your child will love putting his or her miniature stuffed dog inside its very own doghouse!
A child-size handle makes it easy for little ones to carry their furry friend wherever they go!

Skill Level

Intermediate

Materials

- *2 sheets 7-count plastic canvas*
- *J. & P. Coats plastic canvas yarn Article E.46 as listed in color key*
- *DMC 6-strand embroidery floss as listed in color key*
- *#18 tapestry needle*
- *Nylon thread*
- *Kelly green self-adhesive Presto felt from Kunin Felt*

Instructions

1. Cut plastic canvas according to graphs (below and page 42). Cut one 40-hole x 29-hole piece for house bottom. Cut felt slightly smaller than house bottom.

2. Stitch pieces following graphs, working uncoded background on sign with white Continental Stitches. Bottom will remain unstitched.

3. When background stitching is completed, Backstitch letters on sign with 6 strands black floss; Straight Stitch grass on front, back and sides with emerald green and paddy green.

4. Overcast sign with yellow, window edges on sides with emerald green and doorway on house front with black.

5. Using black through step 6, Whipstitch wrong sides of handle pieces together along inside edges and along sides and top of outside edges, leaving bottom edges unstitched at this time. Overcast around side and bottom edges of roof pieces.

6. With wrong sides facing, Whipstitch top edges of roof pieces together, attaching bottom edges of handle where indicated with two stitches per hole while Whipstitching.

7. Center and sew sign above doorway with nylon thread. With bright red, Overcast top edges of front, back and sides. With cardinal, Whipstitch sides to front and back.

8. Center roof evenly on house. Using nylon thread and beginning at top point on house front, sew roof to house along entire top edge of house.

9. Remove paper from felt and attach to house bottom. With felt side up, Whipstitch bottom to house with paddy green, Overcasting doorway edge on bottom while Whipstitching.◆

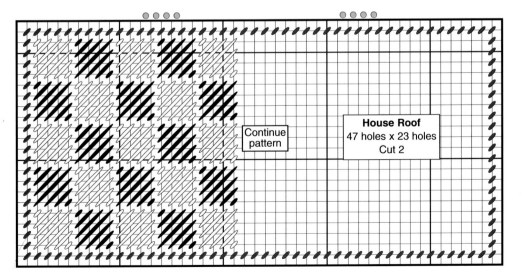

Continue pattern

House Roof
47 holes x 23 holes
Cut 2

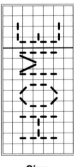

Sign
14 holes x 7 holes
Cut 1

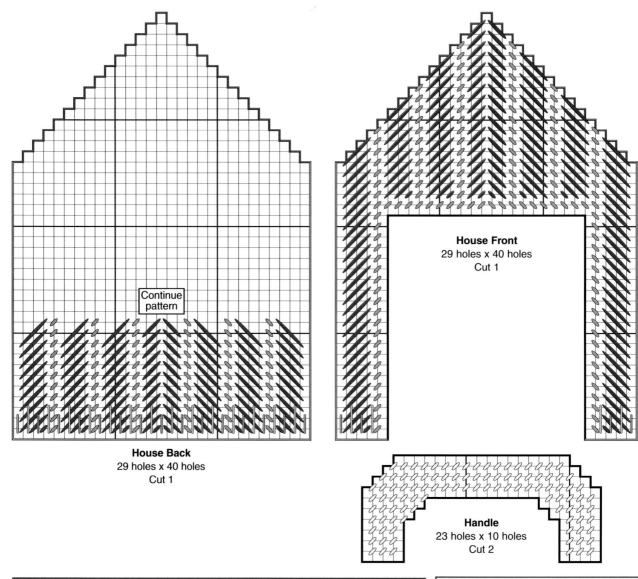

House Back
29 holes x 40 holes
Cut 1

Continue pattern

House Front
29 holes x 40 holes
Cut 1

Handle
23 holes x 10 holes
Cut 2

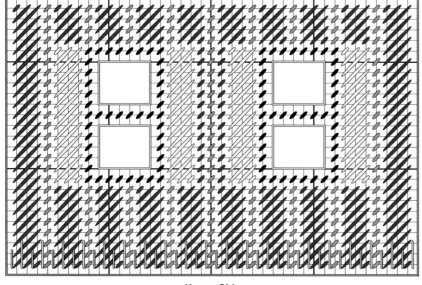

House Side
40 holes x 26 holes
Cut 2

COLOR KEY

Plastic Canvas Yarn	Yards
☐ White #1	16
■ Black #12	20
☐ Yellow #230	10
■ Bright red #901	29
▨ Cardinal #917	16

Uncoded background on sign
is white #1 Continental Stitches

⟋ Emerald green #676 Straight Stitch
and Overcasting   5

⟋ Paddy green #686 Straight Stitch
and Whipstitching   5

6-Strand Embroidery Floss

⟋ Black #310 Backstitch

● Attach handle

Color numbers given are for J. & P. Coats plastic
canvas yarn Article E.46 and DMC 6-strand
embroidery floss.

template, cut perforated paper to match.

2. Following graph, Backstitch and Overcast cone part of piece with one strand gold/gold. For ice cream part of piece, work Cross Stitches with double strand black/coal black, then Continental Stitch and Overcast remainder of piece with double strand coral rose/pink metallic.

3. Spread craft glue on white side of perforated paper; place on backside of stitched piece. Allow to dry.

4. Attach key ring with coral rose/pink metallic to top of cone where indicated on graph.

5. With small length of gold/gold, work several Straight Stitches at back of cone from blue dot to blue dot to bend canvas in shape of a cone.◆

Ice Cream Cone **Key Ring**

Design by Mary T. Cosgrove

Want to keep your child from losing his or her house key?
Why not attach it to this "totally cool" key ring?

Skill Level

Beginner

Materials

◆ Small amount Uniek Quick-Count 10-count plastic canvas

◆ Rayon metallic Shimmer-Blend RibbonFloss by Rhode Island Textile Co. as listed in color key

◆ #18 tapestry needle

◆ 25mm silver split key ring

◆ Small amount 14-count gold metallic perforated paper

◆ Craft glue

Instructions

1. Cut plastic canvas according to graph. Using ice cream cone as a

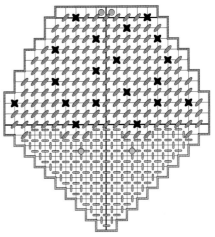

Ice Cream Cone
20 holes x 21 holes
Cut 1

COLOR KEY	
Rayon Metallic Ribbon Floss	**Yards**
■ Coral rose/pink metallic #148F-30	5
■ Black/coal black metallic #148F-34	2
⟋ Gold/gold metallic #148F-21 Backstitch and Overcasting	3
● Attach key ring	
Color numbers given are for Rhode Island Textile Shimmer-Blend Ribbon Floss.	

Southwest Pencil Holder instructions begin on page 46

Tepee **Bank**

Design by Ronda Bryce

While sitting on a bookshelf, it will look just like a decoration.
Much to your child's delight, this tepee is really a bank!

Skill Level

Beginner

Materials

◆ 1 sheet 7-count plastic canvas

◆ 6" plastic canvas radial circle

◆ Spinrite plastic canvas yarn as listed in color key

◆ #16 tapestry needle

◆ 3 (3⁄16" x 10") wooden dowels

Project Note

Tepee is designed as a coin bank. Paper money will be difficult to remove. Coins can be removed by turning bank upside down and shaking them out of the top.

Instructions

1. Cut plastic canvas according to graph.

2. Stitch tepee following graph, working uncoded area with taupe Continental Stitches. Overcast long straight top edge with walnut. Plastic canvas circle will remain unstitched.

3. Folding top edge, overlap piece just enough to make bottom of tepee the size of plastic canvas circle. *Note: Top edge of tepee has now become front of tepee.* With walnut, Whipstitch tepee bottom to circle, working two stitches in each hole and also working through all three thicknesses at the front.

4. With walnut, tack front of tepee together 2⅛"–2¼" from top. Using photo as a guide, place three dowels inside tepee and tack to top with walnut yarn. ◆

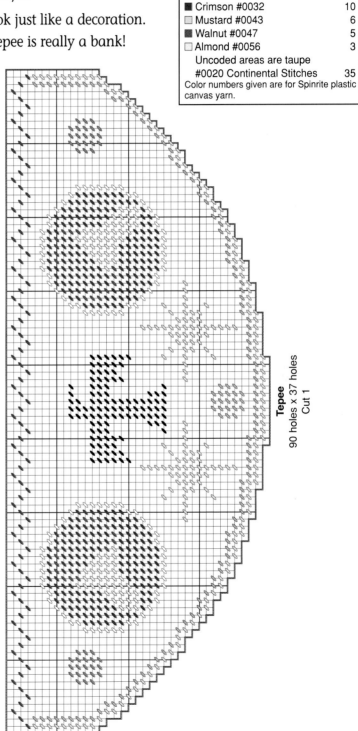

COLOR KEY

Plastic Canvas Yarn	Yards
☐ Wine #0011	4
◼ Royal #0026	2
◼ Black #0028	3
◻ Orange #0030	5
◼ Crimson #0032	10
☐ Mustard #0043	6
◼ Walnut #0047	5
☐ Almond #0056	3
Uncoded areas are taupe	
#0020 Continental Stitches	35

Color numbers given are for Spinrite plastic canvas yarn.

Tepee
90 holes x 37 holes
Cut 1

Southwest Pencil Holders

Design by Ronda Bryce • See photo on page 44

For home or at school, these guy's and gal's pencil holders are sure to delight your hard-to-please kids!

Skill Level

Beginner

Materials

- ◆ *2 sheets 7-count plastic canvas*
- ◆ *4 (3") plastic canvas radial circles by Uniek*
- ◆ *Spinrite plastic canvas yarn as listed in color key*
- ◆ *#16 tapestry needle*
- ◆ *33 (5mm) silver beads*
- ◆ *32" 2mm dark brown imitation leather cord*
- ◆ *Sewing needle*
- ◆ *Gray and turquoise sewing threads to match yarns*
- ◆ *Hot-glue gun*

Instructions

1. Cut plastic canvas according to graphs. Cut one 55-hole x 4-hole lid rim for each holder.

2. For each lid top, cut the outermost row of holes from one circle. For each bottom, cut the two outermost rows of holes from one circle.

3. For boy's holder, Continental Stitch one lid rim, one lid top and one holder bottom with rust. Repeat for girl's holder using turquoise.

4. Stitch remaining pieces following graphs, working uncoded areas on boy's holder side with wine Continental Stitches and uncoded areas on girl's holder side with turquoise Continental Stitches. Overcast arrowhead with charcoal, working two stitches in each hole.

5. For boy's holder, using rust and working two stitches in each hole through step 6, Whipstitch long edges of side together and short edges of rim together.

6. Whipstitch lid top to lid rim and holder bottom to side. Overcast bottom edges of rim and top edges of side.

7. Repeat steps 5 and 6 for girl's holder, using turquoise for lid top and rim and using walnut for side and bottom.

Girl's Holder Side
48 holes x 56 holes
Cut 1

8. Center and stitch arrowhead to top of boy's lid with sewing needle and gray thread. Attach beads to top of girl's lid where indicated on bead placement diagram with sewing needle and turquoise thread.

9. Cut imitation leather cord in half. For each holder, insert ends of one cord from outside to inside of holder through holes indicated on side graph. Tie a knot in each end. ◆

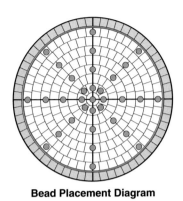

Bead Placement Diagram

COLOR KEY	
BOY'S HOLDER	
Plastic Canvas Yarn	**Yards**
☐ White #0001	2
▨ Natural #0002	5
▨ Curry #0014	4
▨ Charcoal #0021	5
■ Black #0028	6
■ Crimson #0032	3
▨ Rust #0034	26
☐ Mustard #0043	10
☐ Silver gray #0045	3
☐ Beige #0046	3
Uncoded areas are wine #0011 Continental Stitches	10
● Attach imitation leather cord	
Color numbers given are for Spinrite plastic canvas yarn.	

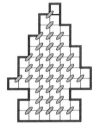

Arrowhead
8 holes x 11 holes
Cut 1

COLOR KEY	
GIRL'S HOLDER	
Plastic Canvas Yarn	**Yards**
▨ Curry #0014	4
■ Scarlet #0022	5
☐ Daffodil #0029	4
▨ Orange #0030	4
▨ Crimson #0032	3
☐ Mustard #0043	4
■ Walnut #0047	14
Uncoded areas are turquoise #0017 Continental Stitches	22
⁄ Turquoise #0017 Whipstitching	
● Attach bead	
● Attach imitation leather cord	
Color numbers given are for Spinrite plastic canvas yarn.	

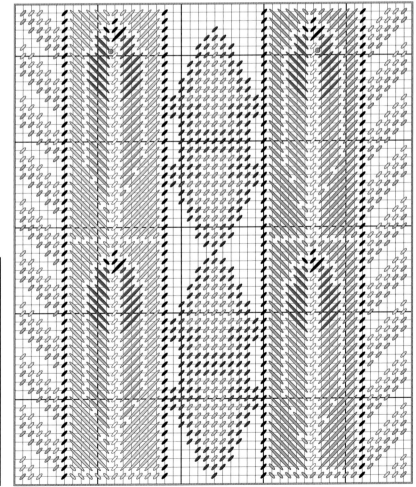

Boy's Holder Side
48 holes x 56 holes
Cut 1

Garage
Bookends

Design by Vicki Blizzard

Your kids will love parking their favorite
miniature cars in this super-cool bookend.

Skill Level
Intermediate

Materials
- 1 sheet Uniek Quick-Count clear 7-count plastic canvas
- 1 sheet Uniek Quick-Count pastel blue 7-count plastic canvas
- Spinrite plastic canvas yarn as listed in color key
- 6" black #00 Uniek Needloft metallic craft cord
- #16 tapestry needle
- 5" metal bookend
- Miniature cars
- Hot-glue gun

Bookend
1. Cut one back and one base from clear plastic canvas and one each from pastel blue plastic canvas according to graphs (right and page 50).

2. Continental Stitch clear pieces following graphs, working uncoded area on back with white Continental Stitches. Pastel blue pieces will remain unstitched.

3. Following graphs and with right sides facing, Whipstitch bottom edge of stitched back to back edge of stitched base.

4. Whipstitch unstitched back to wrong side of stitched back around side and top edges following graph, leaving shelf area unstitched at this time. Slide top of metal bookend between pieces.

5. Following graph and with bottom of metal bookend between pieces, Whipstitch unstitched base to wrong side of stitched base around remaining edges, leaving shelf area unstitched.

Garage Shelf
1. Cut car shelves and garage back, side and roof from clear plastic canvas according to graphs (page 50).

2. Continental Stitch pieces following graphs. Overcast shelves with black.

3. With wrong sides facing and using wine, Whipstitch left side edge of garage back to one side edge of garage side.

4. With silver gray, Whipstitch roof to side and back; Overcast remaining roof edges. With wine, Overcast remaining edges of garage side.

5. With wine, Whipstitch garage back to shelf area on bookend back and base through all three layers.

6. Glue roof to bookend back; glue bottom edge of garage side to bookend base. Using photo as a guide, glue car shelves evenly spaced inside garage.

Gas Pump

1. Cut gas pump pieces, nozzle pieces and gas sign pieces from clear plastic canvas according to graphs (below and page 50).

2. Stitch pieces following graphs, reversing one nozzle before stitching and working uncoded areas on front, back and sign pieces

with white Continental Stitches. Work Backstitches with 2 plies black when background stitching is completed.

3. Using scarlet throughout, Overcast bottom edges of front, back and sides and inside edges on side B. Whipstitch pump front and back to sides, then Whipstitch front, back and sides to top. Whipstitch wrong sides of sign pieces together.

4. With one end of black craft cord between back edges,

Whipstitch wrong sides of nozzle pieces together with silver gray.

5. Thread remaining end of craft cord from front to back through hole indicated on pump side B. Pull through to form a 4"-long hose. Knot securely on wrong side; secure knot with a drop of glue.

6. Using photo as a guide, glue sign to top of pump and pump to almond area on base, making sure side B is facing front. Insert nozzle in pump. Park cars on shelves in garage. ◆

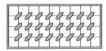

Gas Pump Top
9 holes x 4 holes
Cut 1 from clear

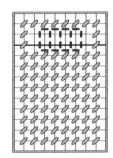

Gas Pump Front & Back
9 holes x 13 holes
Cut 2 from clear

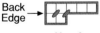

Back Edge →

Nozzle
5 holes x 2 holes
Cut 2, reverse 1, from clear

COLOR KEY

Plastic Canvas Yarn	Yards
☐ Sky #0004	21
◼ Wine #0011	16
◼ Charcoal #0021	2
◼ Scarlet #0022	7
◼ Brisk green #0027	1
◼ Black #0028	34
☐ Daffodil #0029	1
◼ Silver gray #0041	5
☐ Almond #0056	7
Uncoded areas are white #0001 Continental Stitches	3
╱ Black #0028 Backstitch	
● Attach black craft cord	

Color numbers given are for Spinrite plastic canvas yarn.

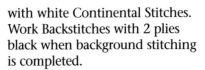

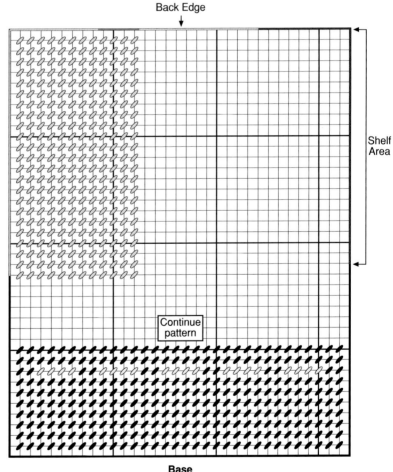

Base
33 holes x 40 holes
Cut 1 from clear
Stitch as graphed
Cut 1 from pastel blue
Do not stitch

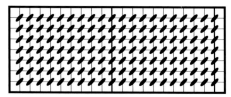

Car Shelf
21 holes x 8 holes
Cut 3 from clear

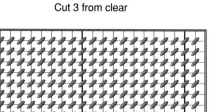

Garage Roof
22 holes x 9 holes
Cut 1 from clear

Gas Sign
8 holes x 7 holes
Cut 2 from clear

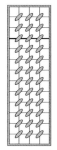

Gas Pump Side A
4 holes x 13 holes
Cut 1 from clear

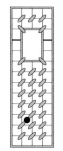

Gas Pump Side B
4 holes x 13 holes
Cut 1 from clear

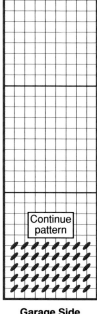

Continue pattern

Garage Side
9 holes x 31 holes
Cut 1 from clear

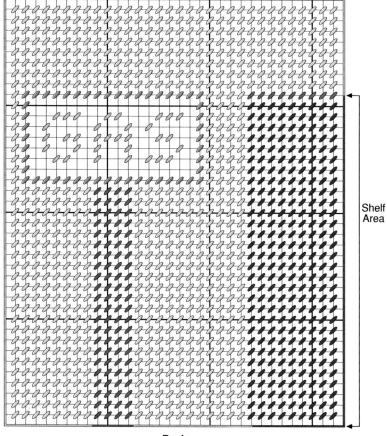

Shelf Area

Back
33 holes x 40 holes
Cut 1 from clear
Stitch as graphed
Cut 1 from pastel blue
Do not stitch

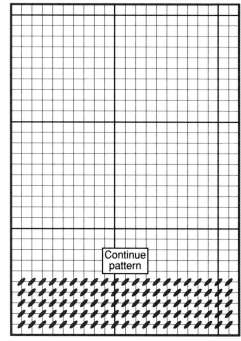

Continue pattern

Garage Back
22 holes x 31 holes
Cut 1 from clear

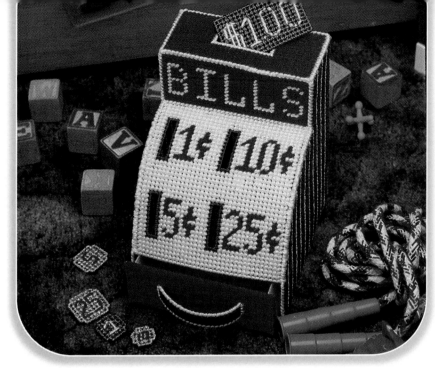

Cash **Register**

Design by Mary T. Cosgrove

Teach your kids about different kinds of money with this red, white and blue cash register. For children under age 4, stitch extra-large plastic canvas coins and bills.

Skill Level
Intermediate

Materials
- 3 sheets Uniek Quick-Count 7-count plastic canvas
- Uniek Needloft plastic canvas yarn as listed in color key
- #16 tapestry needle
- Carat 2mm knitted ribbon braid by Madeira as listed in color key
- 2 (½") silver jingle bells (optional)
- Hot-glue gun

Project Note
Jingle bells should not be used for younger children.

Cash Register
1. Cut sides, top, bottom, back, upper front and middle front from plastic canvas according to graphs (pages 52 and 53).

2. Stitch pieces following graphs, reversing one side before stitching and working uncoded areas with white Continental Stitches. Work white Straight Stitch on middle front between numbers on "10¢."

3. Overcast inside edges on middle front with royal and inside edges on top with white.

4. Use photo as a guide and follow Fig. 1 for assembly. With wrong sides facing in and using white through step 6, Whipstitch back edges of sides to long edges of back. Whipstitch top piece to top edges of back and sides.

5. Whipstitch top edge of middle front to bottom edge of upper front. Whipstitch top edge of upper front to remaining edge of top piece.

6. Whipstitch side edges of joined upper and middle fronts to front edges of sides. Whipstitch bottom edges of sides and back to bottom piece. Overcast remaining edges.

Drawer & Money
1. Cut drawer front, handle, coins and dollar bill from plastic canvas according to graphs (page 52).

2. Cut two 42-hole x 12-hole pieces for drawer sides, one 34-hole x 12-hole piece for drawer back and one 34-hole x 42-hole

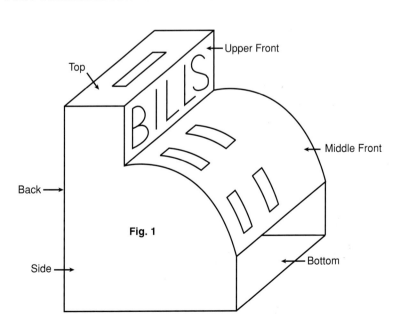

Fig. 1

piece for drawer bottom.

3. Stitch coins, dollar bill, handle and drawer front following graphs. Drawer sides, back and bottom will remain unstitched.

4. Work Backstitches and Straight Stitches on money pieces when background stitching is completed. Overcast coins and dollar bill with adjacent colors.

5. Using white throughout, Overcast long edges of handle. Using two stitches in each hole, Whipstitch short edges of handle to drawer front where indicated on graph with blue lines, attaching

bells if desired to backside while Whipstitching.

6. Using Christmas red and following Fig. 2 through step 8, Whipstitch drawer sides to drawer back along short edges. Whipstitch bottom to back and sides.

7. Whipstitch remaining edge on drawer bottom to bottom edge of drawer front between blue dots.

8. Whipstitch remaining short edges of drawer sides to stitches on backside of drawer front. Overcast remaining edges of drawer front.

9. Insert drawer in bottom of cash register. ♦

COLOR KEY	
Plastic Canvas Yarn	**Yards**
■ Christmas red #02	7
▨ Christmas green #28	4
■ Royal #32	52
Uncoded areas are white	
#41 Continental Stitches	46
✎ Christmas red #02 Backstitch	
✐ White #41 Backstitch,	
Straight Stitch, Overcasting	
and Whipstitching	
2mm Ribbon Braid	
▨ Copper #228	1
□ Silver #242	3
Color numbers given are for Uniek Needloft plastic canvas yarn and Madeira Carat 2mm knitted ribbon braid.	

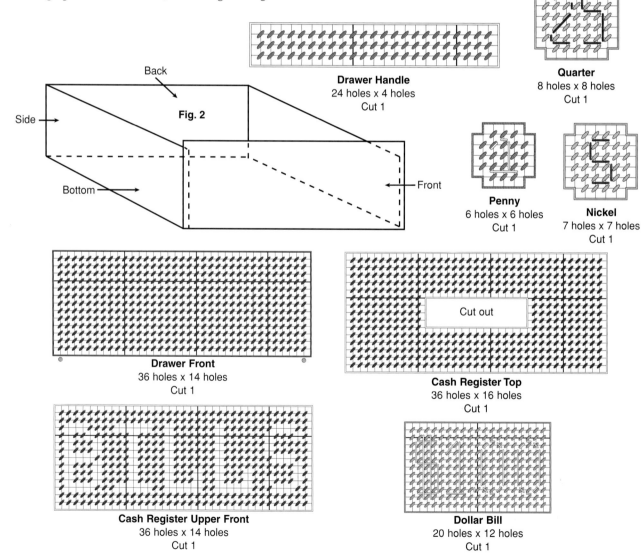

Drawer Handle
24 holes x 4 holes
Cut 1

Quarter
8 holes x 8 holes
Cut 1

Fig. 2
Back
Side
Bottom
Front

Penny
6 holes x 6 holes
Cut 1

Nickel
7 holes x 7 holes
Cut 1

Drawer Front
36 holes x 14 holes
Cut 1

Cut out

Cash Register Top
36 holes x 16 holes
Cut 1

Cash Register Upper Front
36 holes x 14 holes
Cut 1

Dollar Bill
20 holes x 12 holes
Cut 1

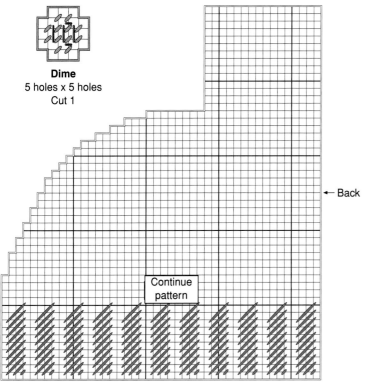

Dime
5 holes x 5 holes
Cut 1

← Back

Continue
pattern

Cash Register Side
44 holes x 50 holes
Cut 2, reverse 1

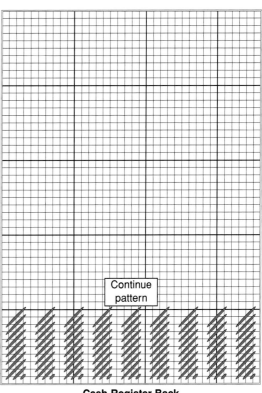

Continue
pattern

Cash Register Back
36 holes x 50 holes
Cut 1

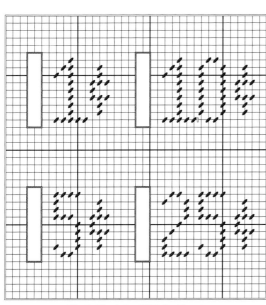

Cash Register Middle Front
36 holes x 38 holes
Cut 1

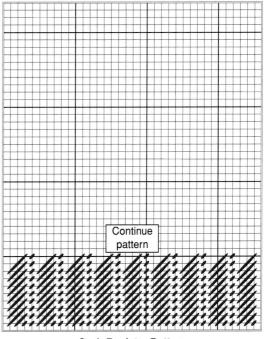

Continue
pattern

Cash Register Bottom
36 holes x 44 holes
Cut 1

The Queen's
Crown & Jewels

Designs by Vicki Blizzard

Delight your little girl by making her queen for a day
with this sparkling crown, cape clip and scepter ensemble!

Skill Level

Beginner

Materials

- 1 sheet Uniek Quick-Count 7-count plastic canvas
- Darice Bright Pearls pearlized metallic cord as listed in color key
- Uniek Needloft metallic craft cord as listed in color key
- #16 tapestry needle
- 9" x 12" sheet white felt
- 14" ¼"-diameter wooden dowel
- Delta Ceramcoat white acrylic paint
- Delta Ceramcoat Sparkle Glaze
- Small paintbrush
- 12" white elastic cord
- 2 (1") spring clothespins from Forster
- Hot-glue gun

Instructions

1. Cut plastic canvas according to graphs.

2. Continental Stitch pieces following graphs. Using adjacent colors, Overcast inside and outside edges of crown; Overcast cape clip and all jewels.

3. With white, Overcast bottom

edges of both heart scepters from dot to dot; Whipstitch wrong sides of scepters together around sides and top from dot to dot.

4. Glue felt to back of crown and cape clip. Allow to dry. Trim felt to fit, cutting out inside holes on crown.

5. Center and glue one large oval jewel to scepter front. Glue one heart jewel to center front of cape clip. Glue clothespins to back of cape clip with clip ends facing out. *Note: To use, clip clothespins to fabric draped around neck.*

6. Paint dowel with two coats of white acrylic paint; allow to dry between coats.

7. When completely dry, paint dowel with two coats sparkle glaze; allow to dry between coats. When completely dry, insert dowel into opening at bottom of scepter; glue in place.

8. Using photo as a guide, glue jewels to crown. Thread ends of elastic cord from front to back through holes indicated on graph. Pull ends to fit child's head; knot on wrong side. Secure knots with a dot of glue. ◆

Small Oval Jewel
4 holes x 5 holes
Cut 6

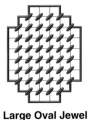

Large Oval Jewel
7 holes x 9 holes
Cut 2

Heart Jewel
7 holes x 7 holes
Cut 2

COLOR KEY

Pearlized Metallic Cord	Yards
☐ White #3410-01	36
Metallic Craft Cord	
■ Red #01	8
● Attach elastic cord	

Color numbers given are for Darice Bright Pearls pearlized metallic cord and Uniek Needloft metallic craft cord.

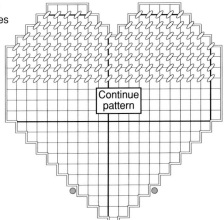

Cape Clip
15 holes x 15 holes
Cut 1

Heart Scepter
21 holes x 21 holes
Cut 2

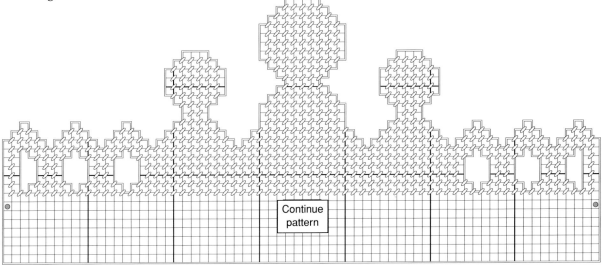

Crown
70 holes x 30 holes
Cut 1

Old MacDonald's Farm

Design by Johnna Miller

Movable animals and a sing-along sun make this a wonderful toy for young
children. Kids will learn their animals while using their imagination at play!

Skill Level

Beginner

Materials

- *2 sheets 7-count plastic canvas*
- *Uniek Needloft plastic canvas yarn as listed in color key*
- *#16 tapestry needle*
- *9 (8mm) round movable eyes with sew-on backs*
- *Old MacDonald Had a Farm electronic music button*
- *6 hook-and-loop dot or square fasteners*
- *Sewing needle and white thread*

Instructions

1. Use one whole sheet for farmyard. Cut cow, chicken, horse, sheep, fish and sun from remaining sheet plastic canvas according to graphs (right and pages 58–59).

2. Stitch farmyard following graph (pages 58 and 59), working uncoded areas below sail blue sky with Christmas green Continental Stitches. Overcast edges with adjacent colors.

3. Stitch remaining pieces following graphs. When background stitching is completed, work black French Knots for noses on cow, horse and sheep; work bittersweet Straight Stitches for beak on chicken.

4. Overcast edges of animals with adjacent colors. Whipstitch wrong sides of sun together with yellow, inserting music button between pieces before closing.

5. Using sewing needle and white thread through step 6, attach eyes to animals where indicated on graphs.

6. Sew soft side of hook-and-loop fasteners to animals and sun, making sure stitching does not show on front side. Attach stiff side of hook-and-loop fasteners to farmyard where indicated on graph. ◆

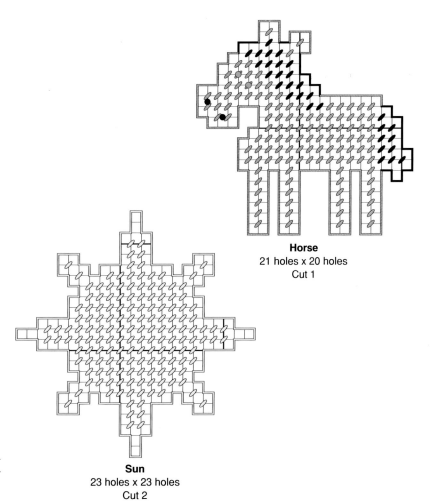

Horse
21 holes x 20 holes
Cut 1

Sun
23 holes x 23 holes
Cut 2

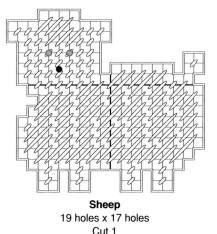

Sheep
19 holes x 17 holes
Cut 1

COLOR KEY	
Plastic Canvas Yarn	**Yards**
■ Black #00	6
■ Red #01	14
☐ Pink #07	1
■ Cinnamon #14	13
■ Christmas green #28	37
☐ Sail blue #35	40
☐ White #41	9
☐ Camel #43	6
■ Dark royal #48	11
■ Bittersweet #52	5
☐ Yellow #57	12
╱ Bittersweet #52 Straight Stitch	
● Black #00 French Knot	
● Attach movable eye	
● Attach hook-and-loop fastener	
Color numbers given are for Uniek Needloft plastic canvas yarn.	

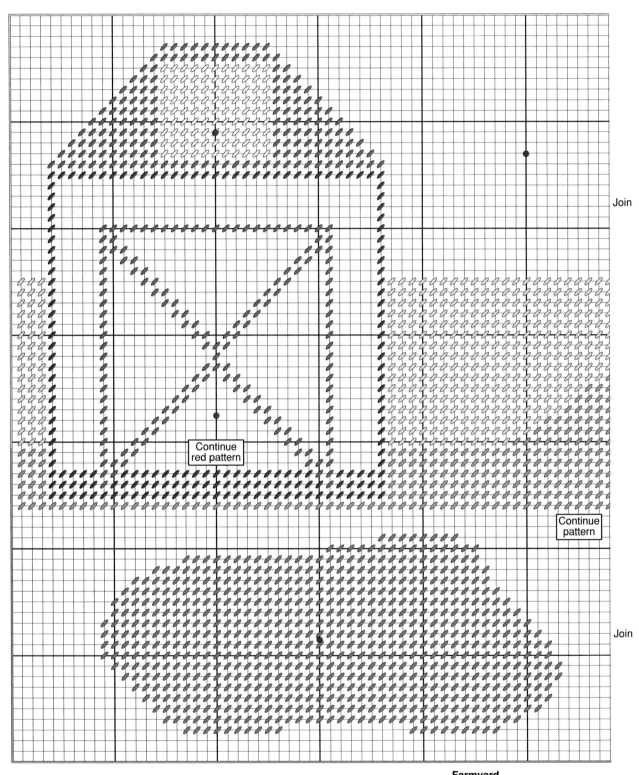

Join

Continue
red pattern

Continue
pattern

Join

Farmyard
90 holes x 70 holes
Stitch 1

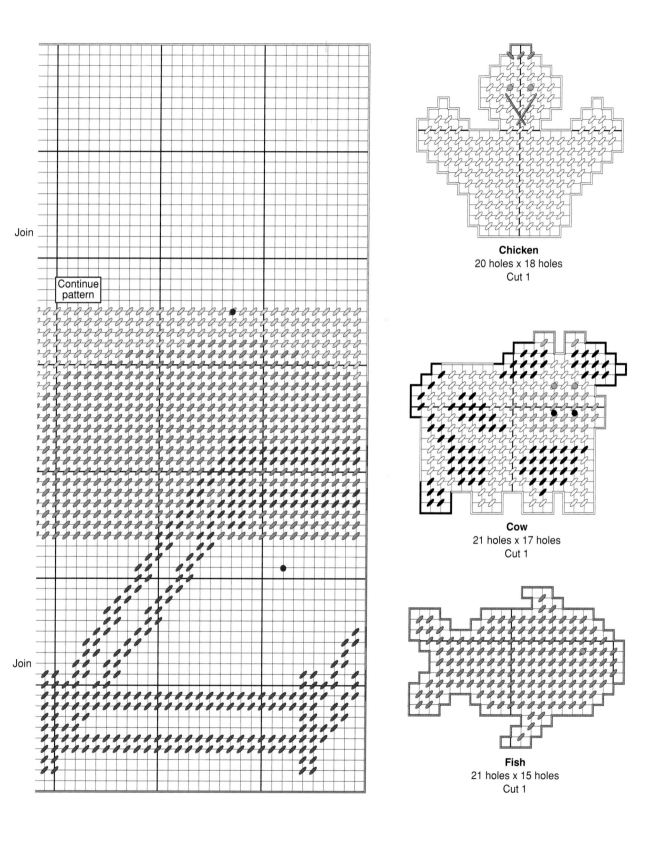

Chicken
20 holes x 18 holes
Cut 1

Cow
21 holes x 17 holes
Cut 1

Fish
21 holes x 15 holes
Cut 1

Join

Continue
pattern

Join

Just for Him

At last—a collection of projects especially designed for men that they'll actually use and appreciate! Choose your husband's favorite colors and create handsome office, den and bedroom accessories to give on a special occasion or just because.

Log Cabin Tissue Topper

Design by Angie Arickx

Stitch this attractive tissue box cover in colors to match your family den or your husband's office. He'll appreciate the masculine touch!

Skill Level
Beginner

Materials
- *1½ sheets 7-count plastic canvas*
- *Uniek Needloft plastic canvas yarn as listed in color key*
- *#16 tapestry needle*

Instructions
1. Cut and stitch plastic canvas according to graphs.

2. Using sandstone throughout, Overcast inside edges of top and bottom edges of sides. Whipstitch sides together, then Whipstitch sides to top. ◆

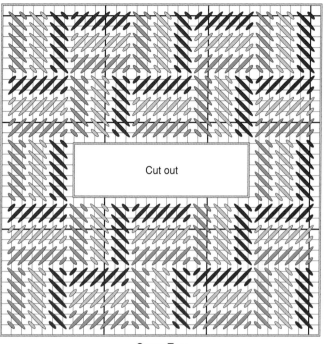

Cover Top
31 holes x 31 holes
Cut 1

Cover Side
31 holes x 37 holes
Cut 4

COLOR KEY	
Plastic Canvas Yarn	**Yards**
■ Burgundy #03	26
□ Sandstone #16	34
■ Teal #50	26
Color numbers given are for Uniek Needloft plastic canvas yarn.	

On Par **Frame**

Design by Carol Nartowicz

Frame a photo of your husband with his golfing
buddies in this dimensional golf-lovers frame!

Skill Level
Intermediate

Materials
- *2 sheets clear 7-count plastic canvas*
- *Small amount black 7-count plastic canvas*
- *Uniek Needloft plastic canvas yarn as listed in color key*
- *DMC 6-strand embroidery floss as listed in color key*
- *#16 tapestry needle*
- *Hot-glue gun*

Cutting & Stitching
1. Cut basket front and basket back from black plastic canvas according to graphs. Basket front and back will remain unstitched.

2. Cut frame front, basket lining, golf bag, golf balls and golf clubs from clear plastic canvas according to graphs, cutting away blue lines on golf clubs.

3. Cut one 48-hole x 48-hole piece for frame back, two 9-hole x 34-hole pieces for frame stand, eight 4-hole x 20-hole pieces for golf bag inserts and one 1-hole x 30-hole piece for golf bag handle from clear plastic canvas. These pieces will remain unstitched.

4. Stitch frame front, basket lining and golf bag following graphs. Work dark mauve Backstitches on golf bag when background stitching is completed.

5. Using silver, stitch and Over-
Continued on pages 66 & 67

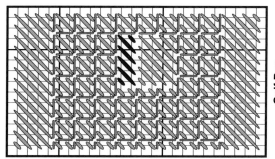

Golf Bag
14 holes x 25 holes
Cut 1 from clear

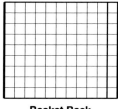

Basket Lining
12 holes x 9 holes
Cut 1 from clear

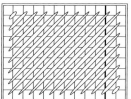

Basket Back
11 holes x 9 holes
Cut 1 from black

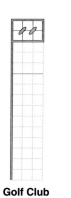

Golf Club
3 holes x 15 holes
Cut 6 from clear,
cutting away blue lines

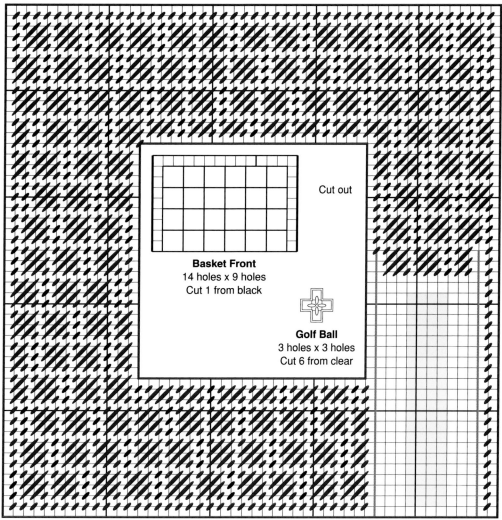

Basket Front
14 holes x 9 holes
Cut 1 from black

Cut out

Golf Ball
3 holes x 3 holes
Cut 6 from clear

On Par Frame Front
48 holes x 48 holes
Cut 1

Catch of the Day
Coaster Set

Design by Niki Russos-Atkinson

This a-lure-ing coaster set makes an eye-catching decoration,
from the vibrant-colored fish to the wicker-look holder.

Skill Level

Intermediate

Materials

- ◆ *4 sheets clear 7-count plastic canvas*
- ◆ *3 sheets brown 7-count plastic canvas*
- ◆ *Darice Nylon Plus plastic canvas yarn as listed in color key*
- ◆ *#16 tapestry needle*
- ◆ *21" 1"-wide webbing*
- ◆ *Hot-glue gun*

Instructions

1. Cut strap holders, latch and creel front, back, top and bottom pieces from brown plastic canvas according to graphs (pages 65—68). Creel bottom, one creel top and one creel back will remain unstitched. Unstitched top and bottom will be used for lining.

2. Cut eight fish coaster pieces from clear plastic canvas according to graph. Four fish will remain unstitched for lining.

3. Stitch latch, front, one back, one top, two strap holders and four fish following graphs. Work vertical Long Stitches on creel pieces first, then work horizontal stitches. Leave bars indicated for attaching strap holders on creel back unstitched at this time.

4. With light aqua, Whipstitch one unstitched fish to wrong side of each stitched fish.

5. Using brown throughout, Overcast top edges of strap holders. Place unstitched back on wrong side of stitched back. Whipstitch side and bottom edges of strap holders to back where indicated on graph.

6. Using maple through step 8, with right side facing out, Whipstitch long straight edge of front to curved side and front

edges of bottom from dot to dot. Overcast top edge of front.

7. With lining on the inside, Whipstitch creel back pieces to back edge of bottom through all three thicknesses. Whipstitch front and back together along side edges through all thicknesses.

8. Place unstitched top lining on wrong side of stitched top; Whipstitch together along inside edges and around curved side and front edges from dot to dot. Whipstitch unstitched back edge of top to unstitched top edge of back through all thicknesses.

9. With brown, Overcast side and bottom edges of latch; Whipstitch top edge of latch to top where indicated on graph. Glue one end of webbing into each strap holder

pocket on creel back. Store coasters in creel. ◆

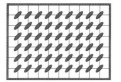

Strap Holder
10 holes x 7 holes
Cut 2 from brown

COLOR KEY	
Plastic Canvas Yarn	**Yards**
▨ Burnt orange #17	8
■ Bittersweet #18	8
☐ Yellow #26	8
▨ Forest green #32	4
▨ Maple #35	36
■ Brown #36	12
☐ Light aqua #39	28
☐ Fern #57	20
╱ Brown #36 Backstitch	
╱ Attach strap holders	
╱ Attach latch	
Color numbers given are for Darice Nylon Plus plastic canvas yarn.	

Fish Coaster
41 holes x 41 holes
Cut 8 from clear
Stitch 4

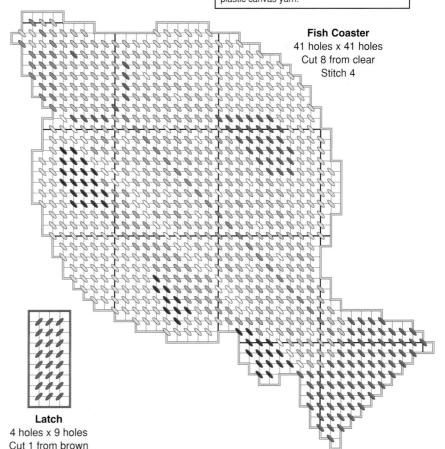

Latch
4 holes x 9 holes
Cut 1 from brown

Back Edge

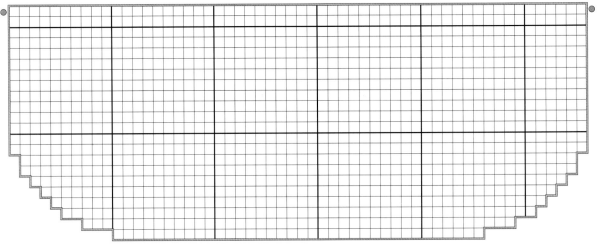

Creel Bottom
56 holes x 22 holes
Cut 1 from brown
Do not stitch

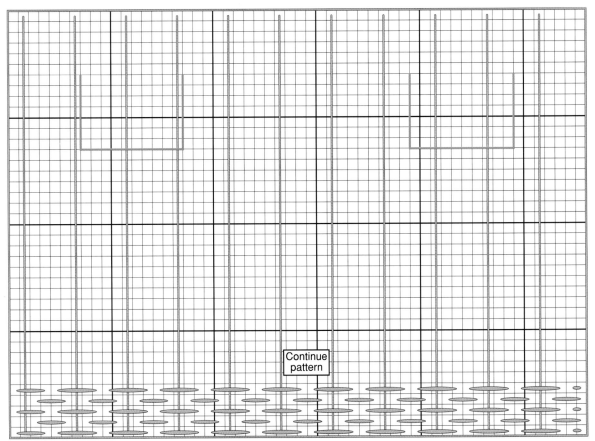

Continue
pattern

Creel Back
56 holes x 40 holes
Cut 2 from brown
Stitch 1

cast golf clubs, reversing two clubs before stitching; wrap and glue yarn around golf club handles.

6. With white, stitch and Overcast golf balls and basket lining.

7. Using burgundy throughout, Overcast golf bag handle and inside edges and top edge of frame front. Whipstitch stand pieces together around two long sides and one short side.

8. With tan, Overcast top and bottom edges of golf bag. With black, Whipstitch side edges of basket front and back together. Do not Overcast top and bottom edges. *Note: Basket front will be curved.*

Assembly

1. Stack inserts together. Center

and baste with tan to area shaded with yellow on unstitched portion of frame front.

2. Use photo as a guide throughout assembly. Using tan, Whipstitch golf bag over inserts to frame front where indicated on graph with blue lines. Glue clubs inside bag.

3. Using burgundy throughout, center and Whipstitch top edge of stand to frame back, making sure bottom edges are even. Whipstitch frame front and back together along side and bottom edges.

4. On right side of golf bag, glue ¾" of front side of one handle end to top of bag. Bend handle down and around and glue 1" of backside on remaining end about 1" above bottom edge of bag.

5. Insert basket lining into basket adjacent to basket front. Glue basket to frame front, making sure bottom edges are even. Glue golf balls together in a cluster as desired to frame front and inside top of basket. ◆

COLOR KEY	
Plastic Canvas Yarn	**Yards**
▨ Burnt orange #17	8
■ Bittersweet #18	8
▢ Yellow #26	8
▨ Forest green #32	4
▨ Maple #35	36
▨ Brown #36	12
▨ Light aqua #39	28
▢ Fern #57	20
✎ Brown #36 Backstitch	
✎ Attach strap holders	
✎ Attach latch	
Color numbers given are for Darice Nylon Plus plastic canvas yarn.	

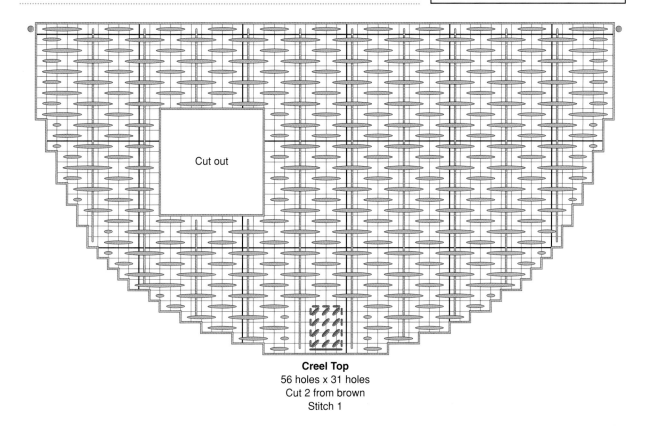

Creel Top
56 holes x 31 holes
Cut 2 from brown
Stitch 1

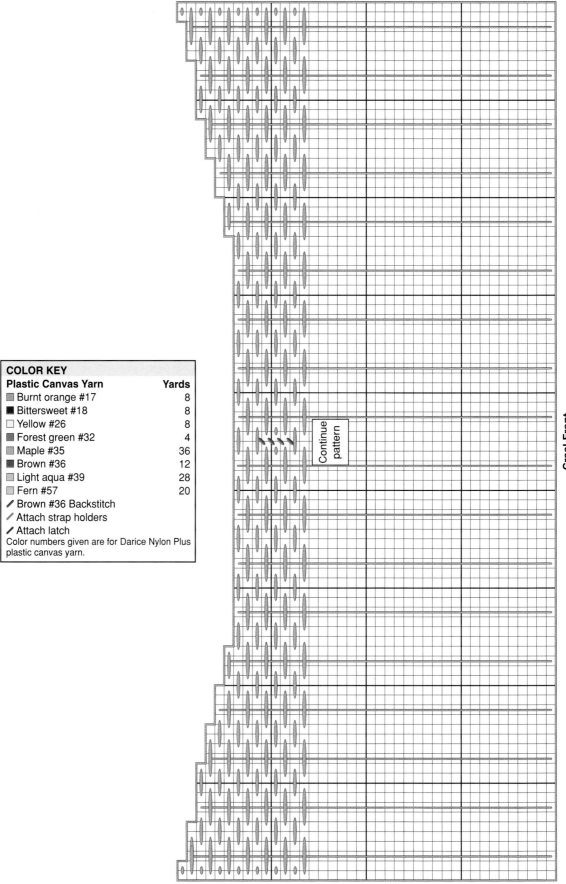

COLOR KEY

Plastic Canvas Yarn	Yards
■ Burnt orange #17	8
■ Bittersweet #18	8
□ Yellow #26	8
■ Forest green #32	4
■ Maple #35	36
■ Brown #36	12
□ Light aqua #39	28
□ Fern #57	20
╱ Brown #36 Backstitch	
╱ Attach strap holders	
╱ Attach latch	

Color numbers given are for Darice Nylon Plus plastic canvas yarn.

Continue pattern

Creel Front
90 holes x 40 holes
Cut 1

Nature's Majesty Frame

Design by Celia Lange Designs

This handsome frame captures the beauty and majesty of the untouched
wilderness. Your husband will enjoy using it to display a favorite photo.

Skill Level

Beginner

Materials

◆ 2 sheets Darice Ultra Stiff 7-count plastic canvas

◆ Red Heart Classic worsted weight yarn Art. E267 as listed in color key

◆ Red Heart Super Saver worsted weight yarn Art. E301 as listed in color key

◆ DMC #3 pearl cotton as listed in color key

◆ #16 tapestry needle

◆ Small plastic, metal or ceramic fish

◆ 1⅝" hand-painted flying eagle button #20457 from JHB International

◆ Pliers

◆ Hot-glue gun

Project Note

Frame holds a 5" x 7" photo.

Instructions

1. Cut plastic canvas according to graphs. Cut one 53-hole x 39-hole piece for frame back.

2. For frame back, with dark sage, work one row of Continental Stitches around entire piece on first bar next to edges, then Overcast edges.

3. Stitch remaining pieces following graphs, reversing one large rock and one small rock before stitching. Work uncoded areas of stream on frame front with blue jewel Continental Stitches. Overcast top edge of stream on frame front with colors indicated while stitching stream.

4. Work black French Knot on bear when background stitching is completed.

5. Overcast bear, pine tree trunks, pine trees and clouds with adjacent colors. Overcast rocks with nickel.

6. For frame front, Overcast inside and outside edges of sky area with light periwinkle. Overcast inside and outside edges of grass area with dark sage. Overcast bottom edge of stream with pale blue.

7. Center frame back on backside of frame front and glue along side and bottom edges, leaving top open to insert photo.

8. Using photo as guide, glue trees, tree trunks, rocks and bear to frame front. Glue fish to bear paw. Using pliers, carefully snap off back of eagle button; glue eagle to sky.

9. Hang as desired. ◆

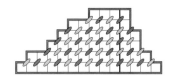

Medium Rock
14 holes x 6 holes
Cut 1

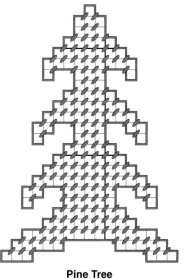

Pine Tree
17 holes x 24 holes
Cut 2

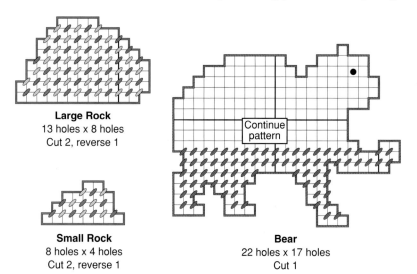

Large Rock
13 holes x 8 holes
Cut 2, reverse 1

Small Rock
8 holes x 4 holes
Cut 2, reverse 1

Continue pattern

Bear
22 holes x 17 holes
Cut 1

COLOR KEY	
Worsted Weight Yarn	**Yards**
☐ White #311	5
■ Brown #328	8
▨ Mid brown #339	2
▨ Light gray #341	5
☐ Light periwinkle #347	19
■ Nickel #401	7
▨ Medium sage #632	17
■ Dark sage #633	24
▨ Pale blue #815	1
Uncoded areas are blue jewel #818 Continental Stitches	1
#3 Pearl Cotton	
● Black #310 French knot	⅛
Color numbers given are for Red Heart Classic worsted weight yarn Art. E267, Red Heart Super Saver worsted weight yarn Art. E301 and DMC #3 pearl cotton.	

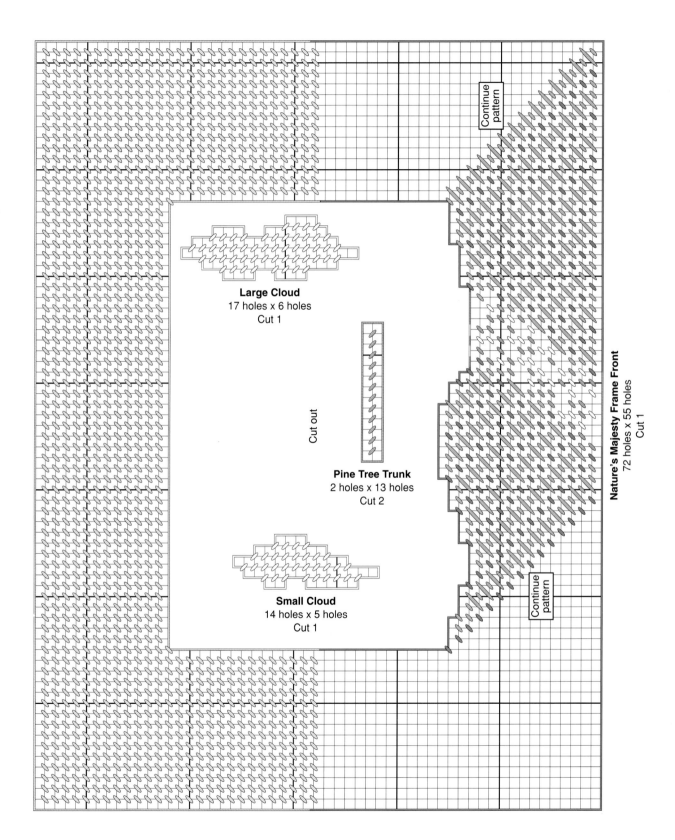

Large Cloud
17 holes x 6 holes
Cut 1

Cut out

Pine Tree Trunk
2 holes x 13 holes
Cut 2

Small Cloud
14 holes x 5 holes
Cut 1

Continue pattern

Continue pattern

Nature's Majesty Frame Front
72 holes x 55 holes
Cut 1

Office Message Center

Design by Mary T. Cosgrove

Whether for his office at home or on the job, your special man can use this message center daily. Tack messages to the cork board, and place business cards and other reminders in the pockets.

Skill Level

Beginner

Materials

- 1½ sheets Uniek Quick-Count clear 7-count plastic canvas
- 1 sheet Uniek Quick-Count pastel yellow 7-count plastic canvas
- Uniek Needloft plastic canvas yarn as listed in color key
- #16 tapestry needle
- 3⅝" x 7⅜" piece heavy-weight paper or brown paper bag
- 3⅝" x 7⅜" piece cork board
- Craft glue

Cutting & Stitching

1. Use one entire sheet clear plastic canvas for message center front and one entire sheet pastel yellow for message center back. Message center back will remain unstitched.

2. From half-sheet of clear plastic canvas, cut pocket fronts according to graph; cut four 4-hole x 14-hole pieces for pocket sides and two 23-hole x 4-hole pieces for pocket bottoms.

3. Following graphs, Continental Stitch pocket pieces and message center front (page 74) with teal and gold, Cross Stitch with crimson and work French Knots with eggshell.

4. Work uncoded areas on bottom and left side of message center front with eggshell Continental Stitches, leaving area indicated for

cork board unstitched and bars for attaching pockets unstitched.

5. Work pocket sides and bottom with teal Continental Stitches.

6. Add gold Straight Stitches when background stitching is completed.

Assembly

1. Use photo as a guide throughout assembly. For each pocket, Whipstitch one short edge of two sides to short edges of one bottom with teal.

2. With gold, Whipstitch sides and bottom to one pocket front; Overcast top edges.

3. With eggshell, Whipstitch unstitched edges of assembled pockets to message center front where indicated on graph.

4. Glue heavy-weight paper, then cork, to message center front where indicated. Allow to dry. *Note: If desired, place wrong side of canvas on waxed paper, then place heavy books on top of cork overnight.*

5. With crimson, Whipstitch sheet of pastel yellow plastic canvas to backside of message center front.

6. Hang as desired. ◆

COLOR KEY	
Plastic Canvas Yarn	**Yards**
☐ Gold #17	11
■ Crimson #42	31
■ Teal #50	43
Uncoded areas are eggshell #39 Continental Stitches	42
⁄ Gold #17 Straight Stitch	
○ Eggshell #39 French Knot	
⁄ Attach pocket	
Color numbers given are for Uniek Needloft plastic canvas yarn.	

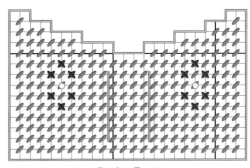

Pocket Front
23 holes x 14 holes
Cut 2 from clear

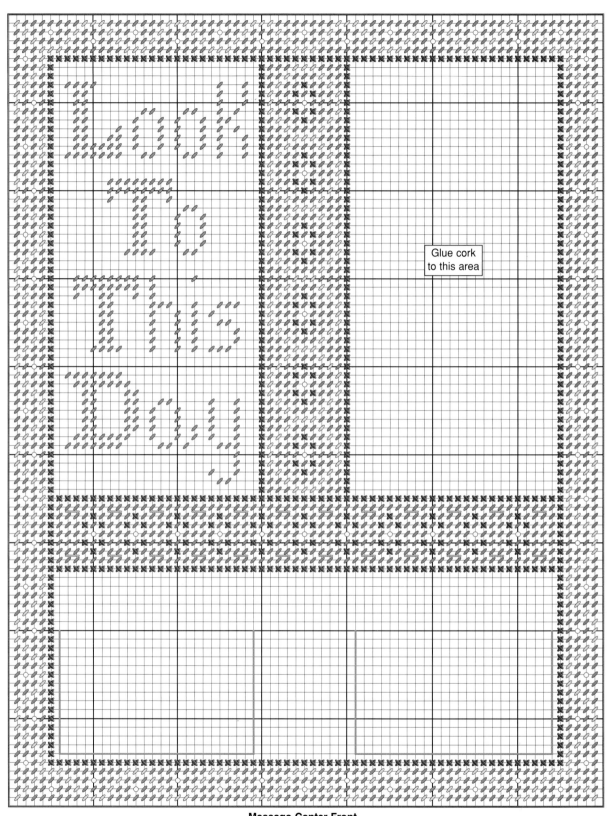

Message Center Front
70 holes x 90 holes
Stitch 1 on clear

Father's Blessing
Sampler

Design by Celia Lange Designs

Honor and delight your father with this inspirational sampler
to remind him of how much you love and appreciate him.

Skill Level

Beginner

Materials

- 2 sheets 7-count plastic canvas
- Red Heart Classic worsted weight yarn Art. E267 as listed in color key
- DMC #3 pearl cotton as listed in color key
- #16 tapestry needle
- Low-temperature glue gun

Instructions

1. Cut plastic canvas according to graphs.

2. Stitch pieces following graphs. When background stitching is completed, work navy blue Back-stitches for lettering on sampler and work cornmeal and honey gold French Knots on bush.

3. Overcast tree with coffee and cloud with white. Overcast bush and inside and outside edges of tree leaves with forest green. Overcast sampler with pale blue and paddy green following graph.

4. Using photo as a guide, glue tree to left side of sampler. Glue leaves over tree, matching upper left corners of leaves and sampler. Glue bush to bottom right corner and cloud along right edge above lettering.

5. Hang as desired. ◆

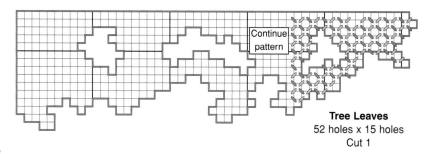

Tree Leaves
52 holes x 15 holes
Cut 1

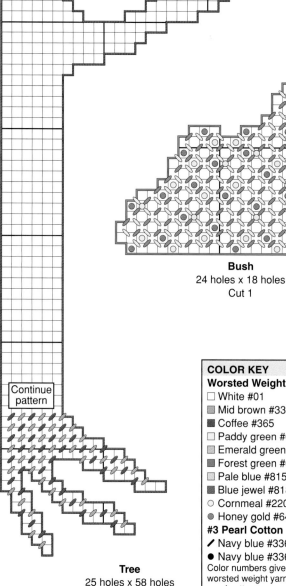

Bush
24 holes x 18 holes
Cut 1

Tree
25 holes x 58 holes
Cut 1

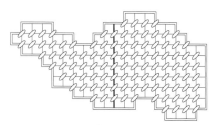

Cloud
19 holes x 10 holes
Cut 1

COLOR KEY	
Worsted Weight Yarn	**Yards**
☐ White #01	5
▨ Mid brown #339	9
■ Coffee #365	15
☐ Paddy green #686	25
▨ Emerald green #676	6
■ Forest green #689	19
▨ Pale blue #815	35
■ Blue jewel #818	34
○ Cornmeal #220 French Knot	3
● Honey gold #645 French Knot	3
#3 Pearl Cotton	
✎ Navy blue #336 Backstitch	8
● Navy blue #336 French Knot	

Color numbers given are for Red Heart Classic worsted weight yarn Art. E267 and DMC #3 pearl cotton.

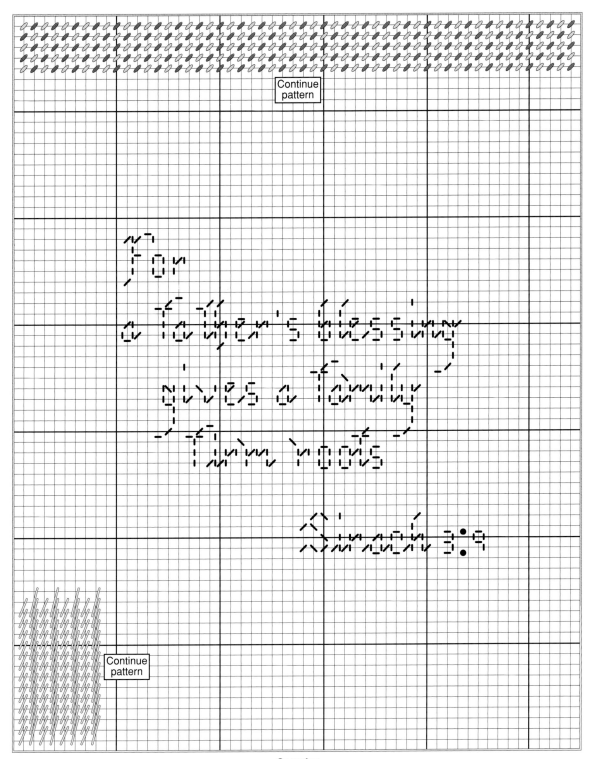

Sampler
55 holes x 69 holes
Cut 1

Medals of Honor
Desk Set

Designs by Ruby Thacker

Validate the bravery and loyalty to our country displayed by a man you respect with this
memorable desk set, including pen and pencil holders, notebook cover and trinket box.

Skill Level
Beginner

Materials
◆ 3½ sheets Uniek Ultra Stiff 7-count plastic canvas
◆ 2 (3") plastic canvas radial circles
◆ Uniek Needloft plastic canvas yarn as listed in color key
◆ Uniek Needloft metallic craft cord as listed in color key
◆ #16 tapestry needle
◆ 3" x 5" memo book with top spiral

Project Note
Remove string from center of craft cord before stitching.

Trinket Box
1. Cut lids and sides from plastic canvas according to graphs (below and page 80).

2. Cut one 40-hole x 39-hole piece for bottom, one 40-hole x 9 hole piece for long divider and one 26-hole x 9-hole piece for short divider from plastic canvas.

3. Stitch lids and sides following graphs, working uncoded areas with forest Continental Stitches. Box bottom and dividers will remain unstitched.

4. Using forest throughout, Overcast one long edge of each divider. Following Fig. 1, Whipstitch one short end of small divider to center bar of long divider; Whipstitch dividers to bottom.

5. With yellow, Whipstitch box short sides to box long sides, then Whipstitch sides to bottom. With forest, tack divider ends to yarn on inside of box, making sure yarn does not show through on right side.

6. Using yellow through step 7, Overcast top edges of long sides, leaving top edges of short sides unstitched at this time.

7. Overcast around one long and two short edges of each lid piece from dot to dot, leaving outside edges unstitched. Whipstitch outside edge of left lid to top edge of short side on left side of box. Repeat with right lid and right side of box.

Notebook Cover
1. Cut notebook cover front and back from plastic canvas according to graph (page 80).

2. Cut one 23-hole x 5-hole piece for cover spine, two 23-hole x 20-hole pieces for inside pockets and one 13-hole x 3-hole piece for pencil loop.

3. Stitch cover front as graphed, working uncoded area with forest Continental Stitches. Work cover back, pencil loop, notebook pockets and spine entirely with forest Continental Stitches.

4. Overcast pencil loop with yellow and one 23-hole edge on each inside pocket with forest.

5. Using yellow through step 7,

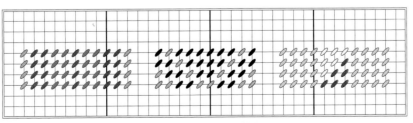

Trinket Box Short Side
39 holes x 10 holes
Cut 2

Whipstitch top edges of front and back to long edges of spine.

6. Matching bottom edges and with wrong sides together, Whipstitch inside pockets to cover front and back, Overcasting remaining cover edges while Whipstitching.

7. Fold pencil loop in half. Through all three thicknesses, stitch short edges of loop to cover back where indicated on cover graph.

8. Insert memo pad covers into pockets of stitched notebook cover.

Pen & Pencil Holders

1. Cut two holders from plastic canvas according to graph.

2. Stitch pieces following graph, overlapping four holes on each holder as indicated before stitching. Work uncoded areas with forest Continental Stitches. 3" plastic canvas circles will remain unstitched.

3. With yellow, Overcast top edge of each holder. Whipstitch one plastic canvas circle to bottom edge of each holder. ◆

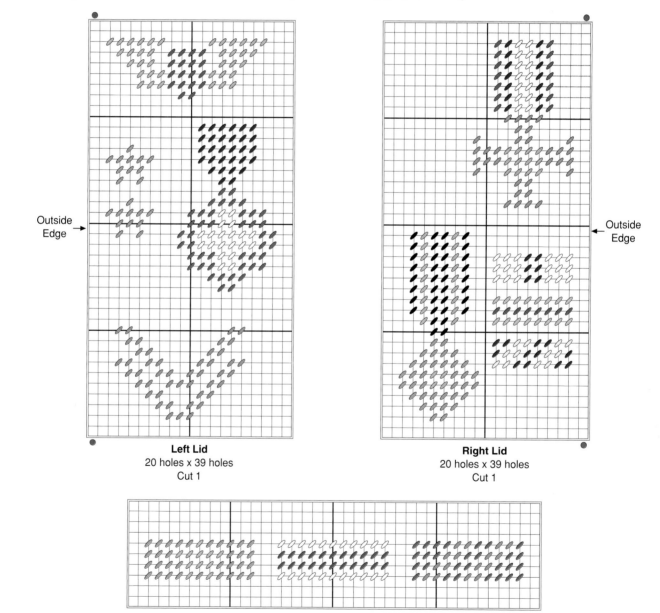

Outside Edge →

← Outside Edge

Left Lid
20 holes x 39 holes
Cut 1

Right Lid
20 holes x 39 holes
Cut 1

Trinket Box Long Side
40 holes x 10 holes
Cut 2

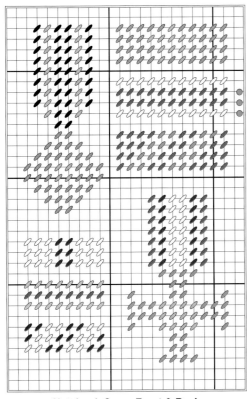

Notebook Cover Front & Back
23 holes x 36 holes
Cut 2
Stitch front as graphed
Stitch back entirely with
forest Continental Stitches

COLOR KEY	
Plastic Canvas Yarn	**Yards**
■ Red #01	5
■ Sundown #10	5
▨ Gold #17	4
▨ Tan #18	3
■ Gray #38	3
□ White #41	4
▨ Dark royal #48	4
□ Yellow #57	18
Uncoded areas are forest	
#29 Continental Stitches	87
Metallic Craft Cord	
▨ Solid gold #20	4
□ Solid silver #21	5
● Attach pencil loop	
Color numbers given are for Uniek Needloft	
plastic canvas yarn and Needloft Craft Cord.	

Fig. 1

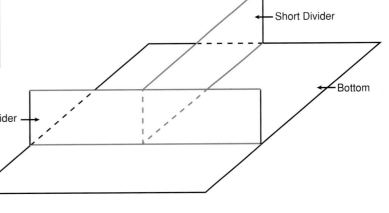

Short Divider

Long Divider

Bottom

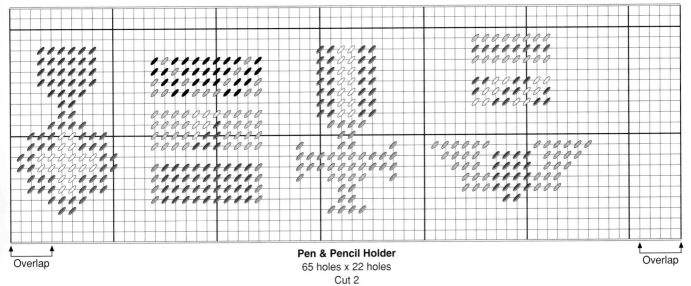

Overlap

Overlap

Pen & Pencil Holder
65 holes x 22 holes
Cut 2

Just for Her

Delight a dear friend with an enchanting and feminine gift to please her eyes and warm her heart. From a beautiful vanity set to a charming potpourri birdhouse, these projects and more make wonderful gifts for Mom, Sis, Grandma or anyone extra-special.

Potpourri **Birdhouse**

Design by Joan Green

This angelic birdhouse makes a delightful addition to the bed or bath.
Fill it with potpourri and give it to a friend for a heavenly scented gift!

Skill Level

Beginner

Materials

- ◆ *1 sheet 7-count plastic canvas*
- ◆ *Spinrite Bernat Berella "4" worsted weight yarn as listed in color key*
- ◆ *1/16"-wide Plastic Canvas 10 Metallic Needlepoint Yarn by Rainbow Gallery as listed in color key*
- ◆ *1/8"-wide Plastic Canvas 7 Metallic Needlepoint Yarn by Rainbow Gallery as listed in color key*
- ◆ *#16 tapestry needle*
- ◆ *28" 1/8"-wide white satin ribbon*
- ◆ *White adhesive-backed felt*
- ◆ *Potpourri*

Instructions

1. Cut plastic canvas according to graphs (also see page 95), cutting out hole on birdhouse front only. Cut one 21-hole x 21-hole piece for birdhouse bottom. Cut felt to fit birdhouse bottom.

2. Stitch pieces following graph, leaving a portion of each wing unstitched as shown on graphs. Stitch entire birdhouse back with established pattern. Birdhouse bottom will remain unstitched.

3. With 1/16"-wide metallic needle-point yarn, work Backstitches and French Knots on roof pieces and Straight Stitches on wings. Work French Knots on front; do not add French Knots to back.

4. With 1/8"-wide metallic needle-point yarn, Overcast inside edges on front; Overcast wings following graphs.

5. With winter white, Whipstitch top edges of roof pieces together; Overcast remaining edges.

6. Using baby blue throughout, Overcast inside edges on sides. Whipstitch front and back to sides, then Whipstitch front, back and sides to bottom. Overcast top edges of front, back and sides.

7. Cut white satin ribbon in half. Thread ends of one length from front to back over peak at top of roof where indicated on one side of roof. Repeat with remaining length of ribbon on other side of roof.

8. Thread ends of ribbon from back to front through holes indicated on birdhouse front and back. Tie ribbons in a bow and trim ends.

9. Insert unstitched portions of wings into slits on house sides. Attach felt to bottom of house. Fill house with potpourri. ◆

COLOR KEY	
Worsted Weight Yarn	**Yards**
☐ Winter white #8941	14
☐ Baby blue #8944	26
1/16" Metallic Needlepoint Yarn	
╱ Gold #PM51 Backstitch and Straight Stitch	8
○ Gold #PM51 French Knot	
1/8" Metallic Needlepoint Yarn	
╱ Gold #PC1 Overcasting	2
● Attach white satin ribbon	
Color numbers given are for Spinrite Bernat Berella "4" worsted weight yarn and Rainbow Gallery Plastic Canvas 7 Metallic Needlepoint Yarn and Plastic Canvas 10 Metallic Needlepoint Yarn.	

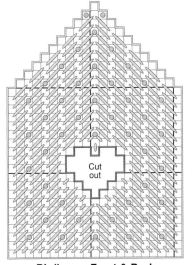

Birdhouse Front & Back
21 holes x 30 holes
Cut 2
Cut out opening on front only

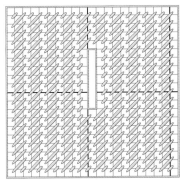

Birdhouse Side
21 holes x 20 holes
Cut 2

Graphs continued on page 95

Love & Dreams

Design by Darla J. Fanton

Inspire a favorite friend with this pretty quilt-style wall hanging.
With its thoughtful sentiment and vibrant colors, it makes a treasured keepsake gift.

Skill Level
Beginner

Materials
◆ *2 sheets Darice Ultra Stiff plastic canvas*
◆ *Spinrite Bernat Berella "4"*

worsted weight yarn as listed in color key

◆ *4 (¾") white buttons*
◆ *1 yard ¼"-wide light blue satin ribbon*
◆ *1½ yards ¾"-wide pre-gathered white eyelet*

◆ *Low-temperature glue gun*

Instructions
1. Cut two pieces plastic canvas according to graph.

2. Holding pieces together, stitch as one, using double strand geranium to stitch heart in center.

3. When background stitching is completed, Backstitch words over border using dark denim. Whipstitch edges together with white.

4. Attach one button in each corner with a geranium Cross Stitch.

5. Cut ribbon in half. Thread ends of one half from front to back through holes indicated on graph.

Fold ends over approximately ½" and glue to backside of ribbon. Tie remaining half in a bow; glue to center of ribbon hanger.

6. Beginning and ending at bottom center, glue bound edge of eyelet around edges of stitched wall hanging on backside, easing lace to fit around corners. ♦

COLOR KEY

Worsted Weight Yarn	Yards
■ Dark denim #8793	16
▨ Pale navy #8836	15
■ Geranium #8929	16
□ Winter white #8941	14

Uncoded areas are winter white #8941 Continental Stitches
╱ Dark denim #8793 Backstitch
● Attach ribbon

Color numbers given are for Spinrite Bernat Berella "4" worsted weight yarn.

Love & Dreams
73 holes x 73 holes
Cut 2, stitch as 1

Stitchin' Caddy

Design by Angie Arickx

From plastic canvas stitchers to quilters, needlecrafters of
all ages will be delighted with this pretty and practical gift!

Skill Level

Intermediate

Materials

- ◆ 1 sheet 10-count plastic canvas
- ◆ DMC #3 pearl cotton as listed in color key
- ◆ DMC 6-strand embroidery floss as listed in color key
- ◆ #18 tapestry needle
- ◆ 10¾" x 7" plastic organizer box
- ◆ Fine sandpaper
- ◆ 2 (5½" x 8¾") Therm O Web PeelnStick double-sided adhesive sheets

Instructions

1. Cut canvas according to graph.

2. Stitch piece following graph, working uncoded areas with white Continental Stitches. Work scalloped edges with white pearl cotton Cross Stitches and Straight Stitches.

3. Work Backstitches with embroidery floss when background stitching is completed. Overcast edges with white.

4. Scuff top of organizer box with fine sandpaper to roughen surface. Cut double-sided adhesive sheets to fit lid on organizer box. Attach sheets to stitched piece and lid, centering stitched piece on lid. Turn caddy upside down on clean surface and place heavy book on box for several hours. ◆

COLOR KEY	
#3 Pearl Cotton	**Yards**
☐ White	82
■ Light blue #813	4
■ Medium blue #826	4
☐ Very light blue #827	5
■ Medium rose #899	10
Uncoded areas are white Continental Stitches	
⁄ White Straight Stitch and Overcasting	
6-Strand Embroidery Floss	
⁄ Rose #335 Backstitch	6
⁄ Dark steel gray #414 Backstitch	9
⁄ Medium blue #826 Backstitch	4
Color numbers given are for DMC #3 pearl cotton and 6-strand embroidery floss.	

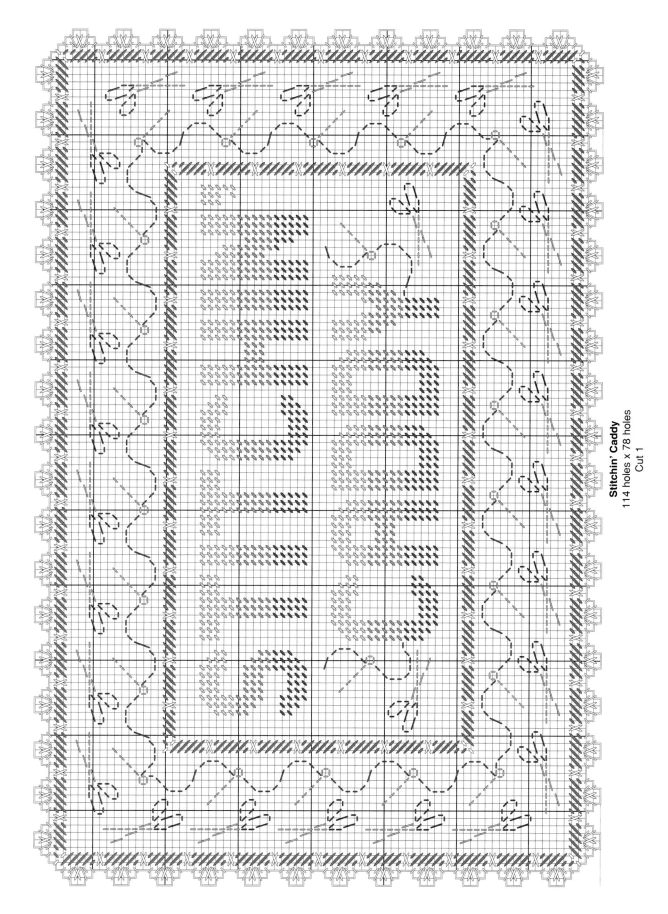

Stitchin' Caddy
114 holes x 78 holes
Cut 1

Materials
- ◆ 1 sheet 7-count plastic canvas
- ◆ Uniek Needloft plastic canvas yarn as listed in color key
- ◆ DMC #3 pearl cotton as listed in color key
- ◆ 1⅓ yards off-white lace
- ◆ ⅔ yard off-white cord

Instructions
1. Cut plastic canvas according to graph.

2. Stitch piece following graph, working uncoded area with eggshell Continental Stitches.

3. When background stitching is completed, with pearl cotton, work French Knots for eyes and flowers and Lazy Daisy Stitches for leaves.

4. Glue lace around edges of stitched sampler on backside. Knot ends of cord. Glue center point of cord to center back of stitched piece along top edge. Tie ends as desired to form a loop for hanging. ◆

Sisters Are Forever

Design by Michele Wilcox

Stitch this special sampler to let your sister know how much you appreciate her.

COLOR KEY	
Plastic Canvas Yarn	**Yards**
■ Black #00	1
▨ Rose #06	10
▨ Cinnamon #14	1
▢ Gold #17	6
▨ Forest #29	7
■ Denim #33	3
▨ Aqua #51	6
▢ Fleshtone #56	2
Uncoded areas are eggshell #39 Continental Stitches	60
⁄ Eggshell #39 Overcasting	
#3 Pearl Cotton	
● Black #310 French Knot	1
◉ Medium terra cotta #356 French Knot	1
○ Dark lemon #444 French Knot	1
⌀ Medium pistachio green #320 Lazy Daisy	1
Color numbers given are for Uniek Needloft plastic canvas yarn and DMC #3 pearl cotton.	

Fancy Hearts
Vanity Set

Design by Angie Arickx

The extra stitching involved in this lovely set will be well worth the effort!
A boutique-size tissue box cover and large vanity tray, worked in lovely
hues of green and pink, make a lovely gift just for her.

Skill Level

Beginner

Materials

- ◆ *3 sheets Darice Ultra Stiff 7-count plastic canvas*
- ◆ *Uniek Needloft plastic canvas yarn as listed in color key*
- ◆ *#16 tapestry needle*

Instructions

1. Cut plastic canvas according to graphs (also see page 92).

2. Stitch pieces following graphs, working uncoded areas with white Continental Stitches.

3. Overcast top edges of tray sides and inside edges of tissue box cover top with white and bottom edges of tissue box cover sides with aqua.

4. Whipstitch tissue box cover sides together with aqua and white following graph, then Whipstitch sides to top with aqua.

5. Whipstitch tray sides together with aqua and white following graph, then Whipstitch sides to bottom with aqua. ◆

COLOR KEY	
Plastic Canvas Yarn	**Yards**
■ Lavender #05	45
□ Pink #07	20
□ Light aqua #49	41
■ Aqua #51	52
Uncoded areas are white #41 Continental Stitches	129
⁄ White #41 Overcasting	
Color numbers given are for Uniek Needloft plastic canvas yarn.	

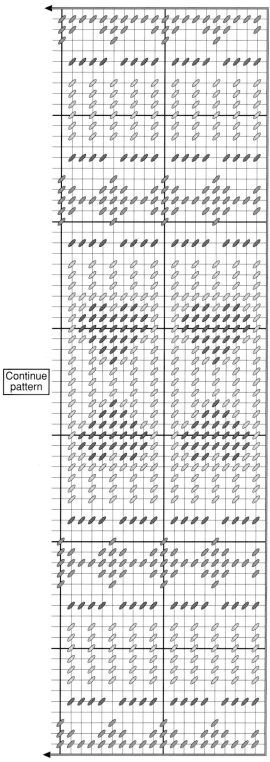

Continue pattern

Vanity Tray Bottom
90 holes x 70 holes
Cut 1

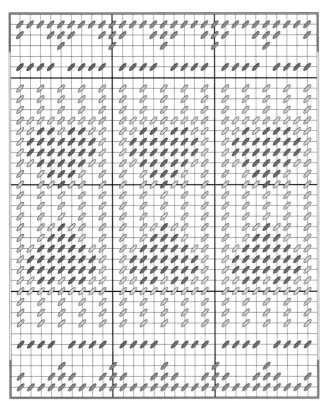

Tissue Box Cover Side
30 holes x 36 holes
Cut 4

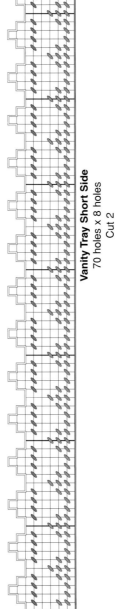

Vanity Tray Short Side
70 holes x 8 holes
Cut 2

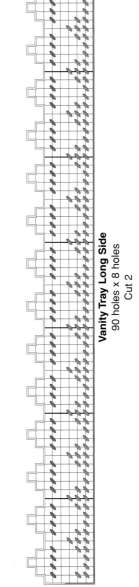

Vanity Tray Long Side
90 holes x 8 holes
Cut 2

COLOR KEY	
Plastic Canvas Yarn	**Yards**
▨ Lavender #05	45
☐ Pink #07	20
☐ Light aqua #49	41
▦ Aqua #51	52
Uncoded areas are white	
#41 Continental Stitches	129
⁄ White #41 Overcasting	

Color numbers given are for Uniek Needloft plastic canvas yarn.

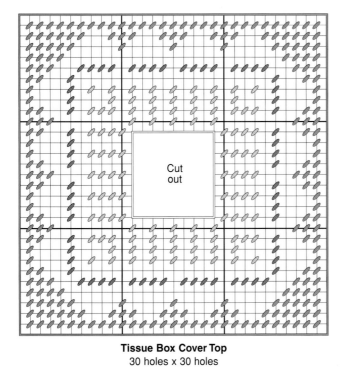

Tissue Box Cover Top
30 holes x 30 holes
Cut 1

Cut out

92 • *Plastic Canvas All-Occasion Gifts*

Chrysanthemum
Organizer

Design by Carol Nartowicz

At home or at the office, this pretty organizer holds a memo pad, personal date book and address book.

Skill Level
Beginner

Materials
- 1 sheet clear 7-count plastic canvas
- 1 sheet yellow 7-count plastic canvas
- Uniek Needloft plastic canvas yarn as listed in color key
- #16 tapestry needle
- Address book approximately 3⅝" x 6¼"
- Personal organizer approximately 3⅝" x 6¼"
- 3" x 5" note pad

Instructions
1. Cut organizer lining pieces from yellow plastic canvas according to graphs (pages 94 and 95). Lining pieces will remain unstitched.

2. Cut front, back and spine from clear plastic canvas according to graphs.

3. Stitch front, back and spine following graphs, working uncoded area on center front with white Continental Stitches. Work embroidery over white Continental Stitches.

4. Place lining pieces on backside of corresponding stitched pieces, making sure inside edges match on front and back pieces and horizontal slit on front lining is at the top.

5. Using baby yellow throughout, Whipstitch inside edges on front to right side of spine through all four thicknesses. Whipstitch inside edges on back to left side of spine through all four thicknesses. Whipstitch lining pieces to stitched pieces around outside edges.

6. Insert note pad in top horizontal slit on front lining. Insert personal organizer and address book in remaining slits. ◆

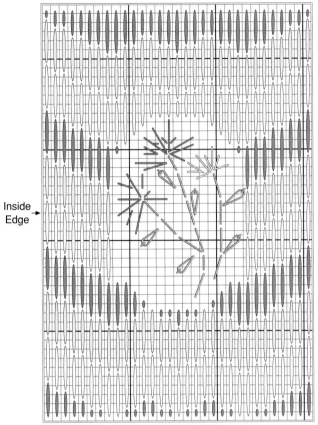

Inside Edge →

Organizer Front
31 holes x 46 holes
Cut 1 from clear

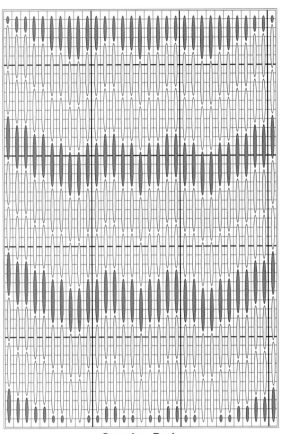

Organizer Back
31 holes x 46 holes
Cut 1 from clear

COLOR KEY	
Plastic Canvas Yarn	**Yards**
■ Tangerine #11	10
☐ Straw #19	10
☐ Baby yellow #21	13
Uncoded area is white #41	
Continental Stitches	6
╱ Tangerine #11 Straight Stitch	
╱ Straw #19 Straight Stitch	
╱ Fern #23 Backstitch	2
◗ Fern #23 Lazy Daisy	
Color numbers given are for Uniek Needloft plastic canvas yarn.	

Organizer Spine
10 holes x 48 holes
Cut 1 from clear
Stitch as graphed
Cut 1 from yellow for lining
Do not stitch

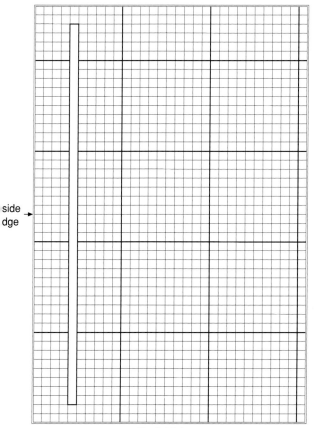

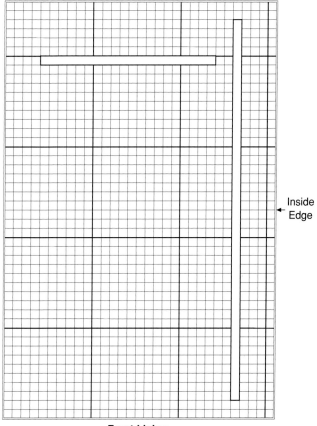

side
dge →

Inside
Edge ←

Back Lining
31 holes x 46 holes
Cut 1 from yellow
Do not stitch

Front Lining
31 holes x 46 holes
Cut 1 from yellow
Do not stitch

POTPOURRI BIRDHOUSE

Continued from page 83

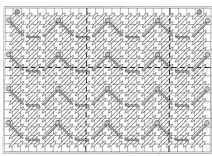

Birdhouse Roof
25 holes x 17 holes
Cut 2

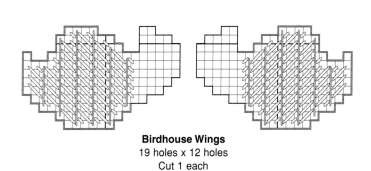

Birdhouse Wings
19 holes x 12 holes
Cut 1 each

For Our Pet Pals

Many of us consider our beloved pet a member of the family, and ever-so-worthy of gifts, too! For those of you with a very soft spot in your heart for your pet, you'll enjoy this collection of practical and decorative gifts for pampering your animal friends!

A Furry Little Christmas

Designs by Vicki Blizzard

Although your dog or cat won't catch the humor of these ornaments, you'll enjoy hanging these whimsical doggie bone and cat treats wreath ornaments on your Christmas tree year after year!

DOGGIE BONE

Skill Level
Intermediate

Materials
- ¼ sheet Uniek Quick-Count 7-count plastic canvas
- Small amount 10-count plastic canvas
- Uniek Needloft plastic canvas yarn as listed in color key
- DMC #3 pearl cotton:
  - 1 yard snow white
  - 1 yard Christmas green #699
- DMC 6-strand embroidery floss as listed in color key
- #16 tapestry needle
- 24" ⅛"-wide red satin ribbon
- 6 (4mm) ruby Austrian glass rhinestones #110-636-09 from National Artcraft
- Polyester fiberfill
- Hot-glue gun

Instructions
1. Cut bones and holly leaves from 7-count plastic canvas according to graphs.

2. Stitch bones and holly leaves with yarn following graphs. Work Straight Stitches on leaves when stitching is completed; Overcast with holly.

3. With beige, Whipstitch wrong sides of bone pieces together, stuffing with fiberfill before closing. Be careful not to pull fiberfill into stitching.

4. From 10-count plastic canvas, cut one name plate 5 holes high and as wide as necessary to fit desired name (see alphabet), leaving one row of Continental Stitches around name and between letters. *Note: Sample used 16-hole x 5-hole piece.*

5. Using pearl cotton, Continental Stitch name plate with snow white, then Overcast edges with Christmas green. With bright Christmas red floss, Backstitch name over completed background stitching, using alphabet given.

6. Center and glue name plate to bone front. Glue three rhinestones to each leaf where indicated on graph, then glue leaves to bone front directly under name plate.

7. Cut ribbon in half. Thread one length from front to back through each hole indicated at top of bone. Knot each length on backside. Tie remaining ends in a bow; trim as desired.

Bone
25 holes x 15 holes
Cut 2 from 7-count

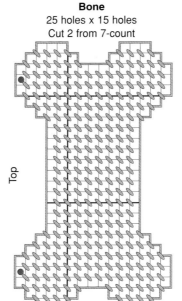

Top

Bone Ornament Alphabet

Holly Leaf
5 holes x 6 holes
Cut 2 from 7-count

CAT TREATS WREATH

Skill Level
Beginner

Materials
- ½ sheet Uniek Quick-Count 7-count plastic canvas
- Uniek Needloft plastic canvas yarn as listed in color key
- DMC 6-strand embroidery floss as listed in color key
- #16 tapestry needle
- 12" ⅛"-wide white satin ribbon
- 2" ⅜"-wide red dotted swiss grosgrain ribbon
- 5" square green felt
- Hot-glue gun

Instructions
1. Cut plastic canvas according to graphs. Cut felt to fit wreath.

2. Stitch and Overcast pieces following graphs. With embroidery floss, work Backstitches, Straight Stitches and French Knots on fish when stitching and Overcasting are completed.

3. Using photo as a guide throughout, tie red dotted swiss ribbon in a bow; cut ends in an inverted "V." Glue to bottom of wreath. Glue angelfish around wreath above bow.

4. Thread ends of white ribbon from front to back through holes on wreath where indicated on graph. Knot ribbon ends, leaving a hanging loop of desired length. Glue felt to backside of wreath. ◆

Angelfish
8 holes x 8 holes
Cut 5

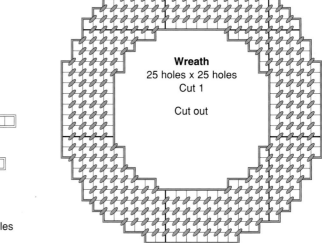

Wreath
25 holes x 25 holes
Cut 1

Cut out

Doggie Treats Jar

Design by Vicki Blizzard

Keep your pooch's special treats in this colorful treat jar. Accented with colorful doggie commands, your pet will quickly recognize this goodie jar!

Skill Level
Beginner

Materials
- 1 artist-size sheet soft 7-count plastic canvas
- 2 (6") plastic canvas radial circles by Uniek
- Uniek Needloft plastic canvas yarn as listed in color key
- DMC #3 pearl cotton as listed in color key
- #16 tapestry needle
- ¼ yard red felt
- ½ sheet white felt
- 5"-diameter x 6½"-tall (26-ounce) coffee can with lid
- Hot-glue gun

Instructions
1. Cut one lid side, one jar side, letters and signs from soft plastic canvas according to graphs (pages 99 and 100).

2. Cut one outside row of holes from one plastic canvas circle for jar bottom. Jar bottom will remain unstitched.

3. Following graphs throughout,

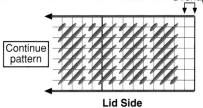

Overlap

Continue pattern

Lid Side
119 holes x 7 holes
Cut 1

stitch lid top (page 100). Overcast letters with royal, working stitches in corners where indicated while Overcasting.

4. Stitch uncoded background on signs with white Continental Stitches; Overcast following graphs. Work Backstitches with black pearl cotton when Continental Stitching and Overcasting are completed.

5. Stitch lid side and jar side following graphs, continuing Slanting Gobelin pattern over three bars. Do not overlap lid side and jar side at this time.

6. Glue white felt to back of stitched lid top and red felt to

back of jar side. Do not glue to unstitched canvas. Allow to dry; trim excess felt.

7. Using Christmas red throughout, roll jar side into a cylinder, overlapping where indicated and placing left edge on top; stitch together with a Continental Stitch. Repeat with lid side. Whipstitch jar side to unstitched jar bottom and lid side to lid top.

8. Using photo as a guide, glue letters to lid top so they read "GOOD DOG TREATS." Glue signs to jar side.

9. Gently insert coffee can into canister, twisting to ease in. Canister fits snugly around can. ◆

COLOR KEY	
Plastic Canvas Yarn	**Yards**
■ Christmas red #02	88
■ Royal #32	11
□ White #41	24
Uncoded areas on signs are white #41 Continental Stitches	
✎ Black #00 Overcasting	2
✎ Holly #27 Overcasting	2
✎ Yellow #57 Overcasting	2
#3 Pearl Cotton	
✎ Black #310 Backstitch	6
Color numbers given are for Uniek Needloft plastic canvas yarn and DMC #3 pearl cotton.	

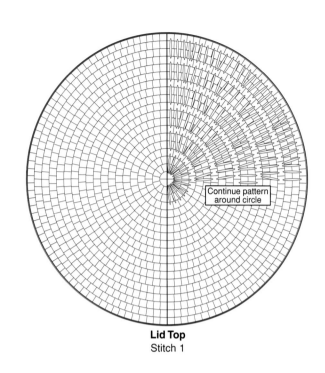

Lid Top
Stitch 1

Lid Letters
5 holes x 7 holes

Cut 2   Cut 3   Cut 2   Cut 2

Cut 1   Cut 1   Cut 1   Cut 1

Jar Signs

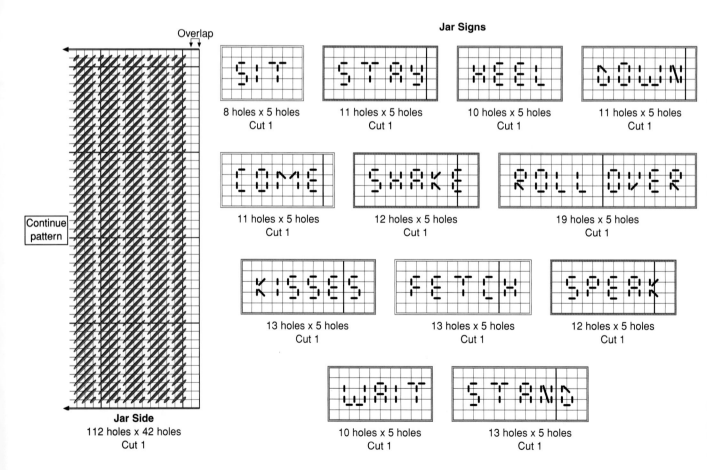

Jar Side
112 holes x 42 holes
Cut 1

8 holes x 5 holes
Cut 1

11 holes x 5 holes
Cut 1

10 holes x 5 holes
Cut 1

11 holes x 5 holes
Cut 1

11 holes x 5 holes
Cut 1

12 holes x 5 holes
Cut 1

19 holes x 5 holes
Cut 1

13 holes x 5 holes
Cut 1

13 holes x 5 holes
Cut 1

12 holes x 5 holes
Cut 1

10 holes x 5 holes
Cut 1

13 holes x 5 holes
Cut 1

Fishy **Frame**

Design by Vicki Blizzard

This fishbowl frame is perfect for framing a photo of your feline friend.

Skill Level
Beginner

Materials
- ½ sheet Uniek Quick-Count clear 7-count plastic canvas
- ½ sheet Uniek Quick-Count pastel green 7-count plastic canvas
- Small amount clear 10-count plastic canvas
- Uniek Needloft plastic canvas yarn as listed in color key
- Kreinik Medium (#16) Braid as listed in color key
- DMC 6-strand embroidery floss as listed in color key
- #16 tapestry needle
- #22 tapestry needle
- Hot-glue gun

Project Note
Use #16 tapestry needle for 7-count and #22 tapestry needle for 10-count.

Instructions
1. Cut one frame front from clear 7-count plastic canvas; cut three fish from clear 10-count plastic canvas according to graphs (page 102).

2. Cut one frame back and two frame supports from pastel green 7-count plastic canvas. Frame back and supports will remain unstitched.

3. Stitch frame front and fish following graphs. With embroidery floss, work Backstitches and French Knots on fish when background stitching is completed.

4. Overcast fish with star yellow and inside edges on frame front with light aqua.

5. With light aqua, Whipstitch longest straight edge on frame supports to frame back where indicated on graph. Whipstitch wrong sides of frame front and back together with adjacent colors.

6. Using photo as a guide, glue fish to frame front. Insert photo through opening in frame back. ◆

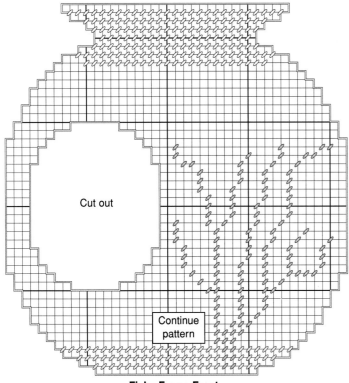

Fishy Frame Front
42 holes x 44 holes
Cut 1 from clear 7-count

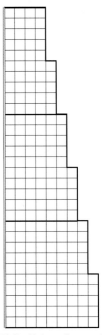

Fishy Frame Support
9 holes x 30 holes
Cut 2 from pastel green 7-count
Do not stitch

COLOR KEY	
Plastic Canvas Yarn	**Yards**
☐ Fern #23	2
☐ White #41	4
☐ Light aqua #49	22
Medium (#16) Braid	
☐ Star yellow #091	5
6-Strand Embroidery Floss	
✒ Black #310 Backstitch	¼
● Black #310 French Knot	
⁄ Attach frame support	
Color numbers given are for Uniek Needloft plastic canvas yarn, Kreinik Medium (#16) Braid and DMC 6-strand embroidery floss.	

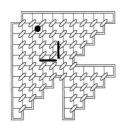

Fishy Frame Fish
10 holes x 10 holes
Cut 3 from clear 10-count

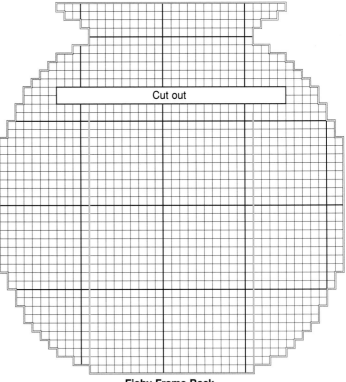

Fishy Frame Back
42 holes x 44 holes
Cut 1 from pastel green 7-count
Do not stitch

Skill Level
Beginner

COOL CAT

Materials
◆ Small amount 7-count plastic canvas

◆ Uniek Needloft plastic canvas yarn as listed in color key

◆ DMC #3 pearl cotton as listed in color key

◆ #16 tapestry needle

◆ ⅝" white 4-hole button

Continued on page 108

COLOR KEY	
COOL CAT	
Plastic Canvas Yarn	**Yards**
Uncoded area is royal #32 Continental Stitches	6
∕ Royal #32 Overcasting	
#3 Pearl Cotton	
∕ White Backstitch and Straight Stitch	2
○ Attach button	
● Attach elastic cord	
Color numbers given are for Uniek Needloft plastic canvas yarn.	

COLOR KEY	
KITTY PRINCESS	
Pearlized Metallic Cord	**Yards**
☐ White #3410-01	2
☐ Yellow #3410-07	4
● Attach 12mm heart bead	
○ Attach 6mm heart bead	
○ Attach button	
● Attach elastic cord	
Color numbers given are for Darice Bright Pearls pearlized metallic cord.	

Quick Stitch
Cat **Collars**

Designs by Vicki Blizzard

Personalize your cat's collar by stitching a one-of-a-kind creation just for him or her!

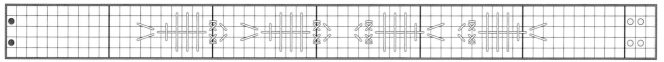

Cool Cat
63 holes x 5 holes
Cut 1

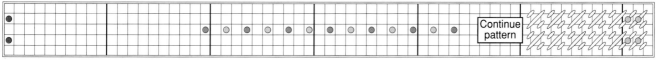

Kitty Princess
63 holes x 5 holes
Cut 1

Continue pattern

Kitty Toys

Designs by Vicki Blizzard

Delight your kitty with these colorful bell cage and curlicue toys!
Make a set for all your friends who are owned by cats!

Skill Level
Beginner

BELL CAGE

Materials
- *Small amount bright blue 7-count plastic canvas*
- *2 (3") plastic canvas radial circles by Darice*
- *Uniek Needloft plastic canvas yarn as listed in color key*
- *#16 tapestry needle*
- *2 (⅝") gold jingle bells*

Instructions
1. For cage ends, cut two plastic canvas circles according to graph, cutting away the five outermost rows of holes and crossbars in center.

2. For bell cage side, cut one 30-hole x 7-hole piece from bright blue plastic canvas. Side will remain unstitched.

3. Using bright blue through step 4, stitch circles following graph. Overcast inside edge.

4. Roll side into a cylinder, overlapping one hole. Stitch together with a Continental Stitch. Whipstitch one circle to each open end of cage side, inserting bells into cage before closing.

KITTY CURLS

Materials
- *Small amounts assorted bright colors 7-count plastic canvas*
- *18-gauge stem wire*
- *¼" dowel*
- *Wire cutters*
- *2 deep coffee mugs*
- *Boiling water*
- *Ice water*

Instructions
1. Cut plastic canvas into 4-hole x 35-hole strips.

2. Holding stem wire in center of plastic canvas strip, wrap strip around dowel, using wire to hold plastic canvas in curls.

3. Pour boiling water into one mug and ice water into second mug.

4. Dip dowel into boiling water for 30 seconds. Immediately immerse dowel into ice water for 30 seconds.

5. Take dowel out of ice water and remove coil from dowel. Carefully remove wire from curled plastic canvas. ◆

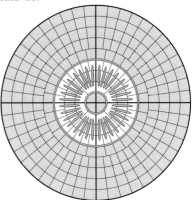

Cage End
Cut 2, cutting away
shaded gray areas

COLOR KEY	
Plastic Canvas Yarn	**Yards**
▢ Bright blue #60	3
Color number given is for Uniek Needloft plastic canvas yarn.	

In the Doghouse Frame
instructions begin on page 108

BEST FRIEND

LET'S GO FOR A
WALK

Pet Leash Hanger instructions begin on page 106

Pet Leash Hanger

Design by Vicki Blizzard • Shown on page 105

Keep your furry friend's leashes close at hand with this whimsical leash hanger!

Skill Level

Intermediate

Materials

- ◆ 1 sheet Uniek Quick-Count clear 7-count plastic canvas
- ◆ ½ sheet lengthwise Uniek Quick-Count royal blue 7-count plastic canvas
- ◆ Uniek Needloft plastic canvas yarn as listed in color key
- ◆ #16 tapestry needle
- ◆ 2 (1") white plastic rings
- ◆ Hot-glue gun

Instructions

1. Cut one hanger base back from royal blue plastic canvas; cut one hanger base front and remaining pieces from clear plastic canvas according to graphs (below and page 107). Back will remain unstitched.

2. Stitch foot and toe pads, hanger base front and peg pieces following graphs.

3. Using dark royal throughout, Overcast foot and toe pads. Overcast letters and apostrophe, working stitches in corners where indicated while Overcasting.

4. Using beige throughout, Whipstitch long edges of four peg sides together. Whipstitch one peg front to one end of assembled peg. Whipstitch remaining open end of peg to one unstitched area on hanger base front. Repeat for second peg.

5. With dark royal, Whipstitch bottom edge of one ring to each upper corner of hanger base back, making sure top edge of ring does not show above top edge of back.

6. With beige, Whipstitch wrong sides of back and front together.

7. Using photo as a guide, glue letters and apostrophe to front, then glue foot and toe pads to front for paw prints following Fig. 1 and photo.

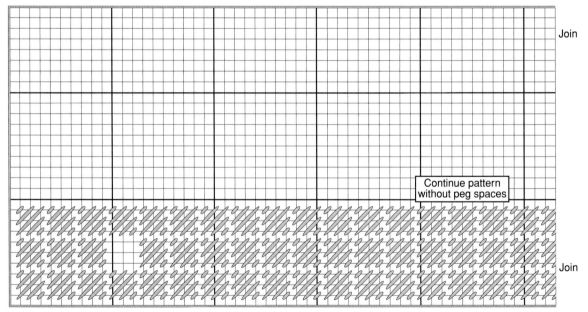

Hanger Base
88 holes x 28 holes
Cut 1 from clear for front
Stitch as graphed
Cut 1 from royal blue for back
Do not stitch

8. Hang pet leashes and collars from pegs. ◆

Hanger Alphabet
5 holes x 7 holes
Cut from clear

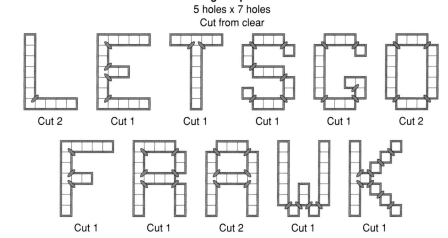

Cut 2   Cut 1   Cut 1   Cut 1   Cut 1   Cut 2

Hanger Apostrophe
2 holes x 3 holes
Cut 1 from clear

Cut 1   Cut 1   Cut 2   Cut 1   Cut 1

Fig. 1

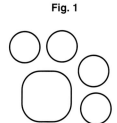

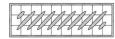

Toe Pad
3 holes x 3 holes
Cut 28 from clear

Foot Pad
5 holes x 5 holes
Cut 7 from clear

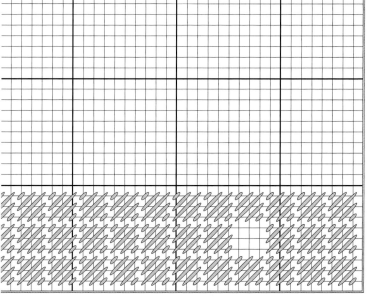

Join

Join

COLOR KEY	
Plastic Canvas Yarn	**Yards**
☐ Beige #40	48
■ Dark royal #48	32
Color numbers given are for Uniek Needloft plastic canvas yarn.	

Peg Side
10 holes x 3 holes
Cut 8 from clear

Peg Front
3 holes x 3 holes
Cut 2 from clear

For Our Pet Pals • **107**

In the Doghouse Frame

Design by Vicki Blizzard • Shown on page 105

Capture your pooch wearing his best smile
in this charming doggie photo frame!

Materials

- ½ sheet Uniek Quick-Count clear 7-count plastic canvas
- ½ sheet Uniek Quick-Count Christmas red 7-count plastic canvas
- Small amount clear 10-count plastic canvas
- Uniek Needloft plastic canvas yarn as listed in color key
- DMC #3 pearl cotton as listed in color key
- DMC 6-strand embroidery floss as listed in color key
- #16 tapestry needle
- #22 tapestry needle
- White felt (optional)
- Hot-glue gun

Project Note

Use #16 tapestry needle for 7-count and #22 needle for 10-count.

Instructions

1. Cut frame front, roof, ball, bone and bowl from clear 7-count plastic canvas; cut sign from clear 10-count plastic canvas according to graphs (page 109).

2. Cut frame back and frame supports from Christmas red 7-count plastic canvas. Frame back and supports will remain unstitched.

3. Stitch and Overcast ball, bone, bowl, roof and sign following graphs, working uncoded area on bowl with royal yarn Continental Stitches and uncoded area on sign with snow white pearl cotton Continental Stitches.

4. Work Backstitches on sign with dark royal blue floss and on bowl with snow white pearl cotton when Continental Stitching is completed.

5. Stitch frame front following graph. Overcast inside edges with white. With Christmas red, Whipstitch longest straight edge on frame supports to frame back where indicated on graph.

6. If desired, cut felt slightly smaller than frame front, cutting out photo opening. Glue felt to backside of frame front.

7. Whipstitch wrong sides of frame front and back together with white.

8. Using photo as a guide, glue roof, sign, ball, bone and bowl to frame front. Insert photo through opening in frame back. ◆

Quick Stitch Cat Collars

Continued from page 103

- 6" white elastic cord
- Seam sealant

Instructions

1. Cut one collar from plastic canvas according to graph (page 103).

2. Continental Stitch uncoded background and Overcast edges with royal. Work embroidery with pearl cotton when background stitching and Overcasting are completed.

3. Attach button with pearl cotton where indicted on graph.

4. Thread elastic through holes indicated, forming a ⅝" loop. Tie in a knot on backside. Secure knot with a drop of seam sealant.

KITTY PRINCESS

Materials

- Small amount 7-count plastic canvas
- Darice Bright Pearls pearlized metallic cord as listed in color key
- #16 tapestry needle
- 6 (6mm) transparent glass heart beads
- 7 (8mm) transparent glass heart beads
- ⅝" yellow 4-hole button
- 6" white elastic cord
- Beading needle and clear thread
- Seam sealant

Instructions

1. Cut one collar from plastic canvas according to graph (page 103).

2. Stitch collar following graph. Overcast with yellow.

3. With beading needle and clear thread, attach beads where indicated on graph, taking two stitches in each bead to secure.

4. Attach button with yellow cord where indicated on graph.

5. Thread elastic through holes indicated, forming a ⅝" loop. Tie in a knot on backside. Secure knot with a drop of seam sealant. ◆

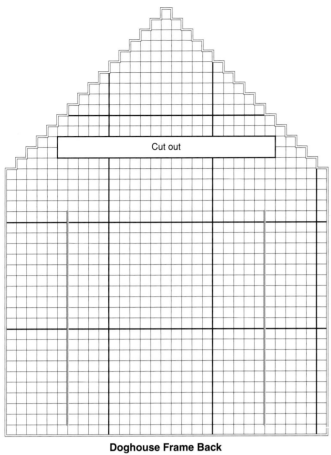

Cut out

Doghouse Frame Back
31 holes x 40 holes
Cut 1 from Christmas red 7-count
Do not stitch

Doghouse Sign
24 holes x 5 holes
Cut 1 from clear 10-count

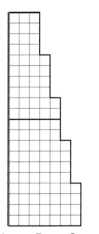

Doghouse Frame Support
7 holes x 20 holes
Cut 2 from Christmas red 7-count
Do not stitch

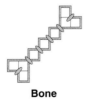

Bone
7 holes x 7 holes
Cut 1 from clear 7-count

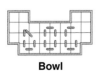

Bowl
8 holes x 4 holes
Cut 1 from clear 7-count

COLOR KEY

Plastic Canvas Yarn	Yards
■ Christmas red #02	5
▨ Beige #40	1
☐ White #41	15
Uncoded area on bowl is royal #32 Continental Stitches	1
⁄ Royal #32 Overcasting	
#3 Pearl Cotton	
Uncoded areas on sign are snow white Continental Stitches	2
⁄ Topaz #725 Overcasting	1
⁄ Snow white Backstitch	
6-Strand Embroidery Floss	
⁄ Dark royal blue #796 Backstitch	1
⁄ Attach frame support	

Color numbers given are for Uniek Needloft plastic canvas yarn and DMC #3 pearl cotton and 6-strand embroidery floss.

Doghouse Roof
28 x 28 holes
Cut 1 from clear 7-count

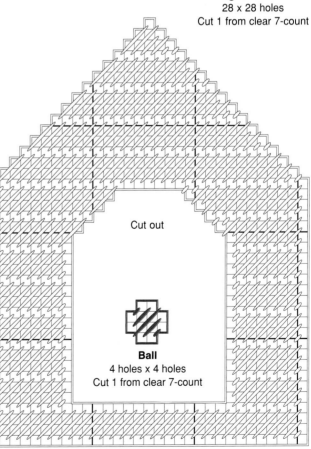

Cut out

Ball
4 holes x 4 holes
Cut 1 from clear 7-count

Doghouse Frame Front
31 holes x 40 holes
Cut 1 from clear 7-count

Celebrate Love

Whether you're stitching a special gift for a wedding, anniversary, Valentine's Day or "just because" occasion, you'll treasure this collection of gifts that say, "Love is in the air!"

Celebrate Love

Pearled Hearts Basket

Design by Vicki Blizzard

Dainty bows and delicate pearls adorn this sweet valentine basket.

Skill Level

Intermediate

Materials

◆ *1 sheet white 7-count plastic canvas*

◆ *⅓ sheet clear 7-count plastic canvas*

◆ *Spinrite plastic canvas yarn as listed in color key*

◆ *#16 tapestry needle*

◆ *1½ yards ⅛"-wide red satin ribbon*

◆ *1 yard ¼"-wide red satin ribbon*

◆ *10 white pearl drops*

◆ *36 (3.5mm) white pearl beads*

◆ *1 sheet white felt*

◆ *Tacky glue*

Cutting & Stitching

1. Cut basket pieces from white plastic canvas and hearts from clear plastic canvas according to graphs. Cut one 39-hole x 27-hole piece from white for basket bottom. Bottom will remain unstitched.

2. For lining, cut felt slightly smaller than basket sides. Set aside.

3. Stitch pieces following graphs. With white, Overcast handle edges and top edges of sides; Overcast only the inside edges indicated on graph.

4. Overcast hearts with scarlet, catching pearl drop while Overcasting hole indicated on graph.

Assembly

1. Cut two 8" lengths and two 6" lengths of ¼"-wide ribbon. Weave 8" lengths through eyelet openings on basket long sides. Weave 6" lengths through eyelet openings on basket short sides. Glue ribbon ends to wrong sides of basket; trim when glue is dry.

2. Cut one 12" length of ⅛"-wide ribbon. Weave through eyelet openings on basket handle. Glue ends to wrong side of basket below handle; trim when glue is dry.

3. Glue felt lining to wrong sides of basket sides.

4. With white, Whipstitch basket short sides to basket long sides, then Whipstitch sides to bottom.

5. Using photo as a guide throughout, glue hearts to sides of basket. Cut remaining ⅛"-wide ribbon into six equal lengths. Tie each length in a small bow; trim ends. Glue one bow to each corner of basket and two bows to basket handle.

6. Glue white pearls to basket where indicated with blue dots. ◆

Pearled Hearts Basket Heart
11 holes x 10 holes
Cut 10 from clear

Pearled Hearts Basket Long Sides & Handle
39 holes x 85 holes
Cut 1 from white

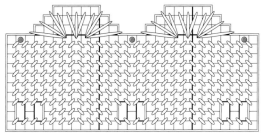

Pearled Heart Basket Short Side
27 holes x 13 holes
Cut 2 from white

COLOR KEY	
Plastic Canvas Yarn	**Yards**
□ White #0001	33
■ Scarlet #0022	10
● Attach pearl drop	
Color numbers given are for Spinrite plastic canvas yarn.	

Lovebirds

Designs by Terry Ricioli

Dress up a corner of your home with this charming three-piece
lovebird set, including a birdhouse, mini-garland and plant poke!

Skill Level

Intermediate

Materials

- *2 sheets 7-count plastic canvas*
- *Uniek Needloft plastic canvas yarn as listed in color key*
- *#16 tapestry needle*
- *1½ yards ⅛"-wide white satin ribbon*
- *5 (5mm) black cabochons*
- *Bamboo skewer*
- *Hot-glue gun*

Birdhouse

1. Cut birdhouse and roof pieces, two birds and two wings from plastic canvas according to graphs (right and page 114), cutting out opening on birdhouse front only.

2. Stitch pieces following graphs, reversing one bird before stitching.

3. Overcast wings with white. Overcast inside opening on front and top edges of birdhouse sides with red. Overcast birds with red and tangerine following graph.

4. Following Fig. 1 throughout assembly and using red through step 5, Whipstitch bottom edges of birdhouse sides together. Whipstitch sides to front and back from bottom point to red dots on graph.

5. Whipstitch top edges of roof pieces together. Whipstitch roof trim front and back to side edges of roof, then Whipstitch top edges of roof trim sides to bottom edges of roof.

6. Using white throughout, Whipstitch roof trim sides to roof trim front and back. Overcast bottom edges of all roof trim pieces.

7. Using photo as a guide, center roof on birdhouse; glue in place. Glue one black cabochon and one wing to each bird. Glue birds to front roof trim.

8. Thread needle with a 12" length of white satin ribbon. Thread ribbon through center holes at peak of roof. Tie ends in a knot to form a loop for hanging.

Garland

1. For garland, cut one of each letter, two birds and two wings from plastic canvas according to graphs (page 114).

2. Stitch and Overcast pieces following graphs, reversing one bird before stitching.

3. Thread remaining ribbon through tops of letters where indicated on graphs; center letters on ribbon.

4. Using photo as a guide, glue ribbon to backside of bird beaks, allowing ends to hang down approximately 2" under beaks. Glue wings and cabochons to birds.

Plant Poke

1. Cut one bird and one wing according to graphs (page 114).

2. Stitch and Overcast pieces following graphs.

3. Glue wing and cabochon to bird. Glue bird to end of skewer. ◆

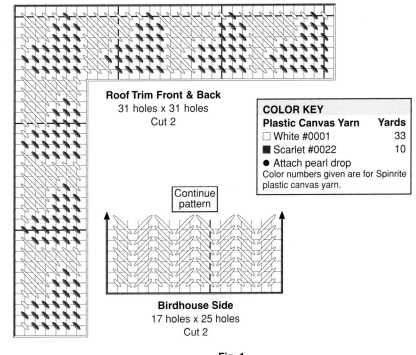

Roof Trim Front & Back
31 holes x 31 holes
Cut 2

Continue pattern

COLOR KEY

Plastic Canvas Yarn	Yards
☐ White #0001	33
■ Scarlet #0022	10
● Attach pearl drop	

Color numbers given are for Spinrite plastic canvas yarn.

Birdhouse Side
17 holes x 25 holes
Cut 2

Fig. 1

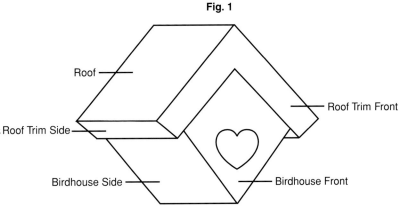

Roof

Roof Trim Side

Birdhouse Side

Roof Trim Front

Birdhouse Front

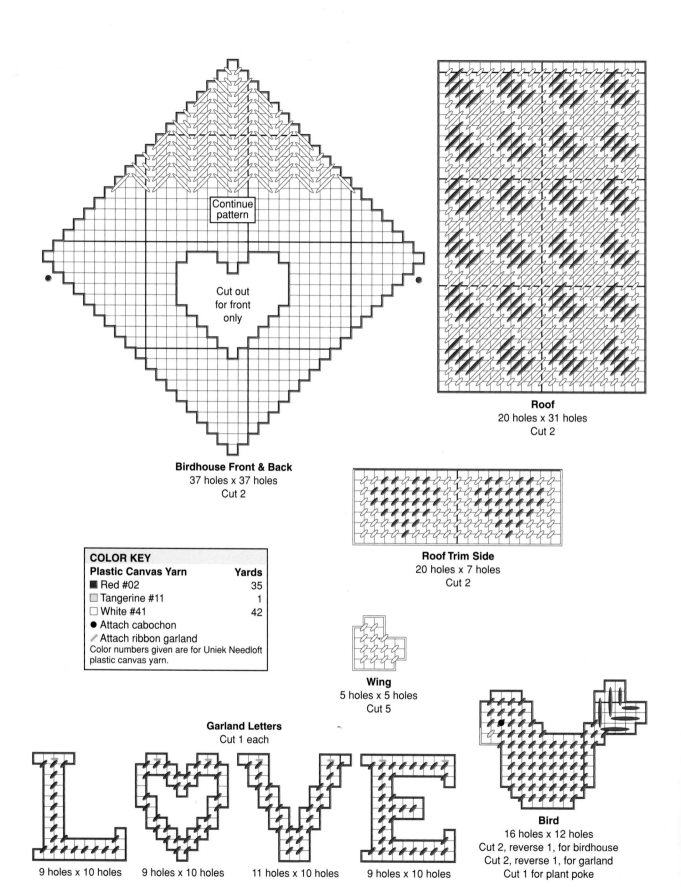

Birdhouse Front & Back
37 holes x 37 holes
Cut 2

Continue pattern

Cut out for front only

Roof
20 holes x 31 holes
Cut 2

Roof Trim Side
20 holes x 7 holes
Cut 2

COLOR KEY

Plastic Canvas Yarn	Yards
■ Red #02	35
▨ Tangerine #11	1
□ White #41	42
● Attach cabochon	
╱ Attach ribbon garland	

Color numbers given are for Uniek Needloft plastic canvas yarn.

Wing
5 holes x 5 holes
Cut 5

Garland Letters
Cut 1 each

9 holes x 10 holes

9 holes x 10 holes

11 holes x 10 holes

9 holes x 10 holes

Bird
16 holes x 12 holes
Cut 2, reverse 1, for birdhouse
Cut 2, reverse 1, for garland
Cut 1 for plant poke

Bridal Suite Door Hanger

Design by Celia Lange Designs

This keepsake door hanger makes a wonderful gift for the bride and groom to use on their honeymoon!

Skill Level

Beginner

Materials

- 1 sheet Darice Ultra Stiff 7-count plastic canvas
- Spinrite plastic canvas yarn as listed in color key
- Kreinik Heavy (#32) Braid as listed in color key
- DMC #3 pearl cotton as listed in color key
- #16 tapestry needle
- 32" ⅜"-wide white satin ribbon
- 1" gold heart
- 4 (1") beaded silver hearts
- 8 small white flowers (sample used beaded flowers)
- Low-temperature glue gun

Instructions

1. Cut plastic canvas according to graph.

2. Cross Stitch hanger with silver and gold following graph, then Continental Stitch uncoded areas with white. When background stitching is completed, Backstitch letters with black pearl cotton. Overcast with white.

3. For hanger, cut a 16" length of white satin ribbon. Thread ends through stitching on backside at top two corners. Make hanger desired length; knot ends to secure and trim excess ribbon.

4. Cut remaining ribbon in half and tie each length in a bow. Using photo as a guide through step 5, arrange gold heart, two silver beaded hearts, five white flowers and one bow at center top of door hanger below gold-and -silver border; glue in place.

5. Arrange remaining silver beaded hearts, flowers and bow at center bottom of door hanger below words and above gold-and-silver border; glue in place. ◆

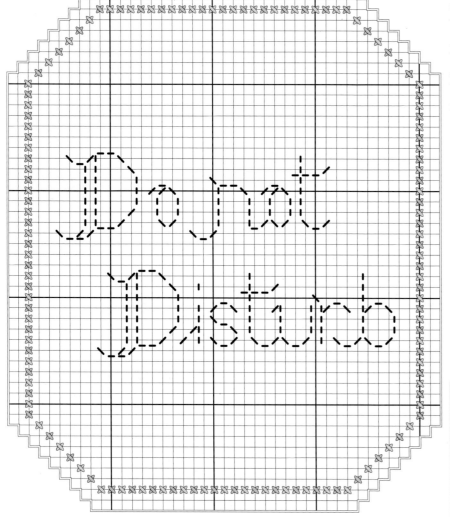

Door Hanger
42 holes x 49 holes
Cut 1

COLOR KEY	
Plastic Canvas Yarn	**Yards**
Uncoded areas are white #0001	
Continental Stitches	33
⁄ White #0001 Overcasting	
Heavy (#32) Braid	
▢ Silver #001	5
▢ Gold #002	5
#3 Pearl Cotton	
✎ Black #310 Backstitch	5
Color numbers given are for Spinrite plastic canvas yarn, Kreinik Heavy (#32) Braid and DMC #3 pearl cotton.	

Kissing in a Tree

Design by Michele Wilcox

Celebrate a couple's engagement with this charming wall decoration.
It makes a heartwarming gift they can look forward to adding to their first home!

Skill Level

Beginner

Materials

◆ *1 sheet 7-count plastic canvas*
◆ *Spinrite Bernat cotton plastic canvas yarn as listed in color key*
◆ *DMC #3 pearl cotton as listed in color key*
◆ *#16 tapestry needle*
◆ *12" jute*
◆ *1 yard green wire*
◆ *Pencil*
◆ *Hot-glue gun*

Cutting & Stitching

1. Cut plastic canvas according to graphs.

2. Stitch pieces following graphs, working uncoded background on hanger with off-white Continental Stitches. Overcast heart and hanger with French blue.

3. Using pearl cotton throughout, work embroidery for heart on tree, shoe straps, mouth and eyes.

4. Use letters given in alphabet to personalize hanger. Count number of bars needed for each letter in names and in the word "and," allowing one bar between letters and two bars between words.

5. With black pearl cotton, center and Backstitch names desired in area shaded with blue. Stitch remaining words following graph.

Finishing

1. Use photo as a guide throughout finishing. For jump rope, thread ends of jute from front to back where indicated below hands, then thread from back to front where indicated at top part of hands. Pull ends until jump rope is desired length. Knot ends at top of hands; trim excess.

2. Cut three 8" lengths of lemon yarn. Place lengths together and fold in half. Braid yarn from fold to desired length; tie off with lemon yarn.

3. Thread a 4" length of yarn through loop at top of braid, then thread ends of 4" length through holes indicated on one side of head. Tie in a knot on backside; trim ends.

4. Repeat steps 2 and 3 for second braid, making sure braids are the same length. Attach braid on opposite side of head where indicated on graph. Trim ends on both braids as desired.

5. Glue heart to girl.

6. Cut wire in half and place lengths together. Thread ends through holes indicated with green dots at top of hanger. Pulls ends through until desired length of loop is reached. Wrap each end around loop close to canvas, then wrap ends around pencil to form spirals. ◆

Kissing in a Tree Heart
5 holes x 5 holes
Cut 1

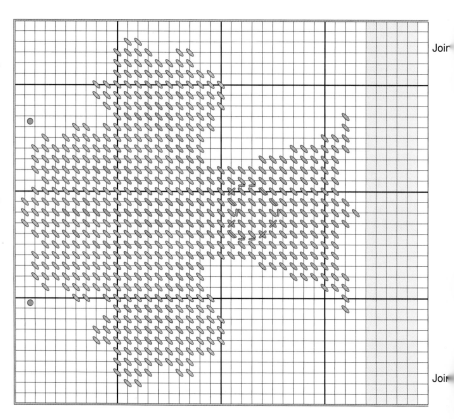

Join

Join

Kissing in a Tree Alphabet

COLOR KEY

Plastic Canvas Yarn	Yards
■ Black #0100	1
□ Flesh #0108	2
▨ Toffee #0111	3
▨ Medium brown #0112	4
□ Lemon #0142	2
▨ Apple green #0145	6
▨ French blue #0147	9
Uncoded areas are off-white #0102 Continental Stitches	60
#3 Pearl Cotton	
✑ Black #310 Backstitch and Straight Stitch	5
✑ Very dark cranberry #600 Backstitch	1
✑ Off-white #746 Backstitch	1
● Black #310 French Knot	
● Dark delft #798 French Knot	1
● Attach jump rope	
○ Attach braid	

Color numbers given are for Spinrite Bernat cotton plastic canvas yarn and DMC #3 pearl cotton.

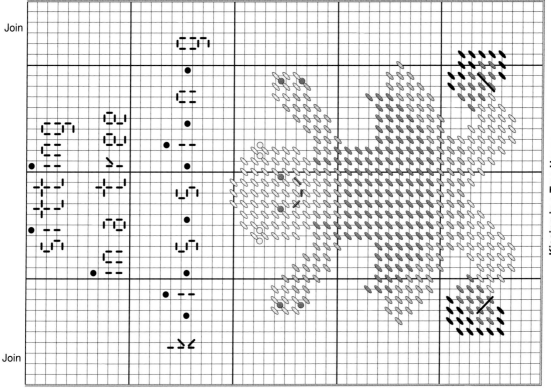

Join

Join

Kissing in a Tree Hanger
36 holes x 90 holes
Cut 1

Welcome Home

Turn a new house into a warm home with this collection of attractive home accessories! Cheerful items for the kitchen, family room, dining room and living room are a pleasure to stitch and a delight to give and share!

Birdhouse Photo *Frame*

Design by Celia Lange Designs

This enchanting frame will add a warm touch to any room in your home.
Use it to capture a favorite family memory!

Skill Level

Intermediate

Materials

- ◆ *2 sheets Darice Ultra Stiff 7-count plastic canvas*
- ◆ *Small amount regular 7-count plastic canvas*
- ◆ *Red Heart Classic worsted weight yarn Art. E267 as listed in color key*
- ◆ *Red Heart Super Saver worsted weight yarn Art. E301 as listed in color key*
- ◆ *#16 tapestry needle*
- ◆ *Assorted white and pink tiny silk flowers*
- ◆ *3 rounded end toothpicks*
- ◆ *3 (1") plastic or resin birds*
- ◆ *Hot-glue gun*

Cutting & Stitching

1. Cut flowerpot pieces from regular plastic canvas; cut remaining pieces from stiff plastic canvas according to graphs (right and pages 122 and 123), cutting out opening on frame front only. Frame back will remain unstitched.

2. Stitch pieces following graphs, working one flowerpot front and one flowerpot back with eggshell as graphed and one each with cornmeal. Work one flowerpot rim with country blue as graphed and one with country rose.

3. Overcast grass, birdhouse roofs, poles and flowerpot rims with adjacent colors. Overcast large bird-house with country rose, medium birdhouse with country blue and small birdhouse with spruce.

4. When background stitching and Overcasting are completed, work Backstitches on medium birdhouse.

5. For flowerpots, using adjacent colors throughout, Overcast top and bottom edges of fronts and backs. Whipstitch side edges of corresponding fronts and backs together, arching fronts.

6. Using cornmeal throughout, Overcast inside edges of frame front and top edges of frame front and back. Whipstitch front to back around side and bottom edges.

Assembly

1. Thread rounded toothpick ends from front to back through bird-houses where indicated on graphs so picks extend approximately ⅜" on fronts; cut off flush with backs. Glue to secure.

2. Using photo as a guide through step 6, glue corresponding roofs to birdhouse tops; glue corresponding poles to birdhouse backs.

3. Glue poles to frame, making sure bottom edges are even. Glue grass to front over poles, making sure bottom edges are even.

4. Glue country blue pot rim to front of eggshell pot along top edge; glue country rose rim to cornmeal pot.

5. Arrange flowers in pots, then feed glue up through bottoms of pots to secure. Glue pots to bottom of frame front, making sure bottom edges are even.

6. Glue one bird to bottom edge of frame front near one flowerpot. Glue remaining birds to toothpick perches of two birdhouses.

7. Hang as desired. ◆

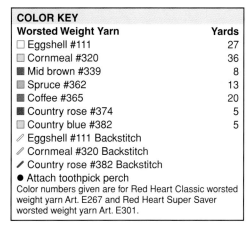

COLOR KEY	
Worsted Weight Yarn	**Yards**
☐ Eggshell #111	27
☐ Cornmeal #320	36
■ Mid brown #339	8
☐ Spruce #362	13
■ Coffee #365	20
■ Country rose #374	5
☐ Country blue #382	5
╱ Eggshell #111 Backstitch	
╱ Cornmeal #320 Backstitch	
╱ Country rose #382 Backstitch	
● Attach toothpick perch	
Color numbers given are for Red Heart Classic worsted weight yarn Art. E267 and Red Heart Super Saver worsted weight yarn Art. E301.	

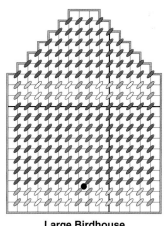

Large Birdhouse
15 holes x 19 holes
Cut 1 from stiff

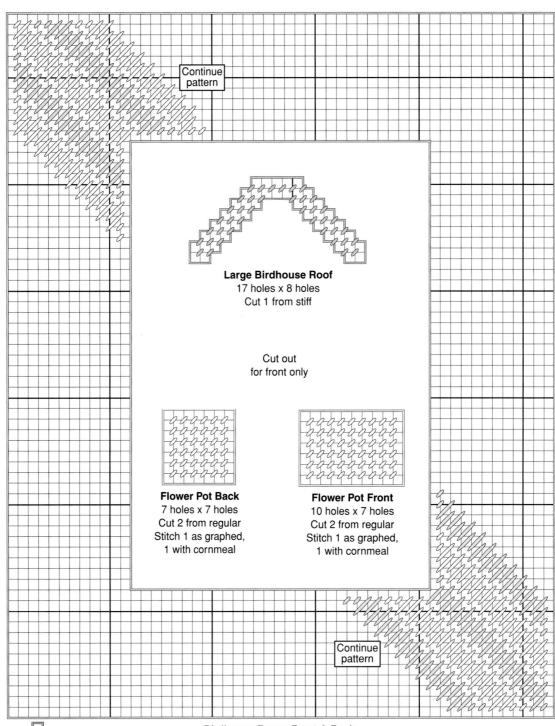

Continue
pattern

Large Birdhouse Roof
17 holes x 8 holes
Cut 1 from stiff

Cut out
for front only

Flower Pot Back
7 holes x 7 holes
Cut 2 from regular
Stitch 1 as graphed,
1 with cornmeal

Flower Pot Front
10 holes x 7 holes
Cut 2 from regular
Stitch 1 as graphed,
1 with cornmeal

Continue
pattern

Birdhouse Frame Front & Back
53 holes x 66 holes
Cut 2 from stiff
Stitch front only

Medium Birdhouse Roof
9 holes x 6 holes
Cut 1 from stiff

Flower Pot Rim
12 holes x 2 holes
Cut 2 from regular
Stitch 1 as graphed,
1 with country rose

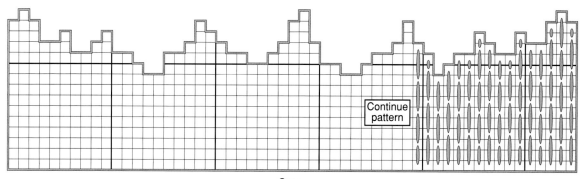

Grass
55 holes x 15 holes
Cut 1 from stiff

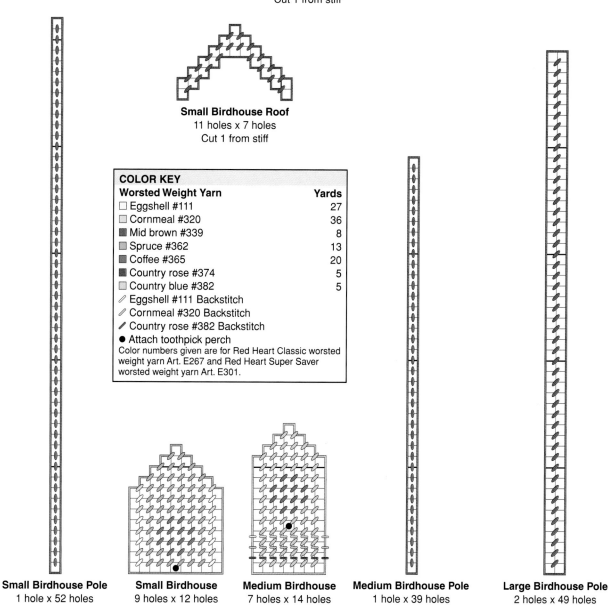

Small Birdhouse Roof
11 holes x 7 holes
Cut 1 from stiff

COLOR KEY

Worsted Weight Yarn	Yards
☐ Eggshell #111	27
☐ Cornmeal #320	36
■ Mid brown #339	8
☐ Spruce #362	13
■ Coffee #365	20
■ Country rose #374	5
☐ Country blue #382	5
╱ Eggshell #111 Backstitch	
╱ Cornmeal #320 Backstitch	
╱ Country rose #382 Backstitch	
● Attach toothpick perch	

Color numbers given are for Red Heart Classic worsted weight yarn Art. E267 and Red Heart Super Saver worsted weight yarn Art. E301.

Small Birdhouse Pole
1 hole x 52 holes
Cut 1 from stiff

Small Birdhouse
9 holes x 12 holes
Cut 1 from stiff

Medium Birdhouse
7 holes x 14 holes
Cut 1 from stiff

Medium Birdhouse Pole
1 hole x 39 holes
Cut 1 from stiff

Large Birdhouse Pole
2 holes x 49 holes
Cut 1 from stiff

Kitchen Cottage

Design by Joan Green

This charming little cottage is just the right size for holding recipe cards,
coupons or other assorted kitchen odds and ends.

Skill Level

Intermediate

Materials

◆ 2 sheets 7-count plastic canvas

◆ Spinrite Bernat Berella "4"
worsted weight yarn as listed in
color key

◆ #16 tapestry needle

Instructions

1. Cut plastic canvas according to
graphs (page 125 and 126). Cut one
46-hole x 26-hole piece for box
base and one 48-hole x 28-hole
piece for roof support. Box base and
roof support will remain unstitched.

2. Stitch remaining roof pieces
following graphs. Work French
Knots on roof edges with 4 plies
pale tapestry gold when background stitching is completed.

3. Work cottage front, back and
sides following graphs. Work
embroidery with 2 plies yarn
when background stitching is
completed.

4. Overcast top edges of cottage
front, back and sides with pale
navy. Whipstitch front, back and
sides together with pale navy and
light sea green following graphs.

5. Whipstitch back and sides to
unstitched bottom with light sea

green; Whipstitch front to bottom
with light sea green and pale
tapestry gold following graph.

6. Using pale tapestry gold
through step 6, Whipstitch top
edges of roof sides to roof top,
then Whipstitch sides together.
Whipstitch unstitched roof support to bottom edges of roof sides.

7. Whipstitch top edge of roof
edge pieces to bottom edge of
roof, working through all three
thicknesses and stitching over
previous Whipstitching.

8. With white, Whipstitch side
edges of roof edges together;
Overcast bottom edges. ◆

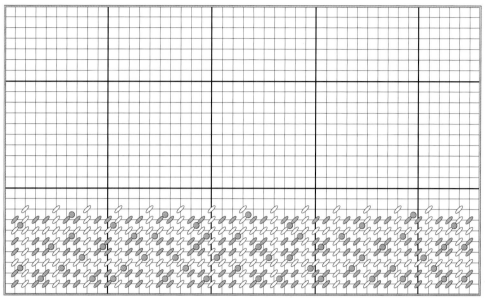

Cottage Back
46 holes x 27 holes
Cut 1

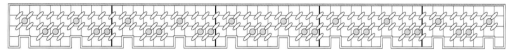

Roof Edge Long Side
48 holes x 4 holes
Cut 2

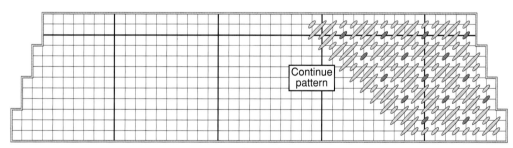

Continue
pattern

Roof Long Side
48 holes x 12 holes
Cut 2

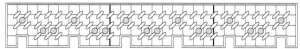

Roof Edge Short Side
28 holes x 4 holes
Cut 2

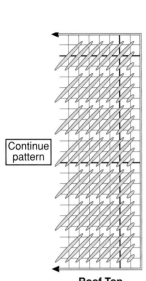

Roof Top
42 holes x 22 holes
Cut 1

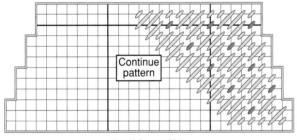

Cottage Front
46 holes x 27 holes
Cut 1

Roof Short Side
28 holes x 12 holes
Cut 2

COLOR KEY	
Worsted Weight Yarn	**Yards**
▨ Antique gold #8810	4
▨ Light sea green #8878	14
☐ Pale tapestry gold #8887	44
▨ Pearl gray #8912	5
☐ White #8942	20
■ Black #8994	4
Uncoded areas are pale navy	
#8836 Continental Stitches	36
╱ Pale navy #8836 Overcasting	
and Whipstitching	
╱ Black #8994 Backstitch	
and Straight Stitch	
● Light pimento #8827 French Knot	4
○ Pale tapestry gold #8887 French Knot	
● Dark peach #8979 French Knot	4
● Black #8994 French Knot	
Color numbers given are for Spinrite Bernat Berella	
"4" worsted weight yarn.	

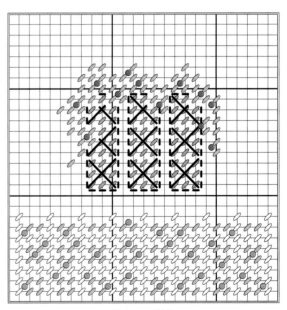

Cottage Side
26 holes x 27 holes
Cut 2

Cottage Doorstop

Design by Michele Wilcox

Celebrate a friend's housewarming by stitching him or her this charming cottage doorstop. They'll appreciate your kindness!

Skill Level
Beginner

Materials
- ◆ 1⅓ sheets 7-count plastic canvas
- ◆ Uniek Needloft yarn as listed in color key
- ◆ DMC #3 pearl cotton as listed in color key
- ◆ #16 tapestry needle
- ◆ Hot-glue gun

Instructions

1. Cut plastic canvas according to graphs (below and page 128). Fences will remain unstitched.

2. Stitch remaining pieces following graphs, working uncoded areas on cottage scene with forest Continental Stitches. Work black pearl cotton French Knot on cottage scene when background stitching is completed.

3. Overcast inside and outside edges of both fences with white. Overcast cottage scene with adjacent colors.

4. Using denim throughout, Overcast bottom edges of sides. Whipstitch sides together, then Whipstitch sides to top.

5. Using photo as a guide and making sure bottom edges are even throughout, center and glue cottage scene to one long side. Glue fences to cottage scene on both sides of door. ◆

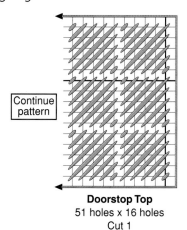

Continue pattern

Doorstop Top
51 holes x 16 holes
Cut 1

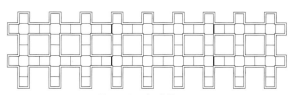

Doorstop Left Fence
27 holes x 7 holes
Cut 1
Do not stitch

COLOR KEY

Plastic Canvas Yarn	Yards
■ Lavender #05	7
■ Sundown #10	2
■ Cinnamon #14	4
□ Mint #24	7
■ Denim #33	60
□ White #41	9
■ Crimson #42	1
■ Mermaid #53	6
□ Yellow #57	2
Uncoded area is forest	
#29 Continental Stitches	7
∕ Forest #29 Overcasting	

#3 Pearl Cotton

● Black #310 French Knot	⅓

Color numbers given are for Uniek Needloft
plastic canvas yarn and DMC #3 pearl cotton.

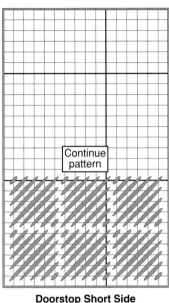

Continue pattern

Doorstop Short Side
16 holes x 26 holes
Cut 2

Continue pattern

Doorstop Long Side
51 holes x 26 holes
Cut 2

Doorstop Right Fence
18 holes x 7 holes
Cut 1
Do not stitch

Cottage Scene
57 holes x 36 holes
Cut 1

Country Plaid
Recipe **Card Box**

Design by Celia Lange Designs

Stitch up this attractive recipe card box in colors to match your kitchen for a warm accent.
The box's slanted lid will keep your card in place while you cook.

Skill Level
Beginner

Materials
- ◆ 2 sheets Darice Ultra Stiff 7-count plastic canvas
- ◆ Red Heart Super Saver worsted weight yarn Art. E301 as listed in color key
- ◆ DMC #3 pearl cotton as listed in color key
- ◆ #16 tapestry needle
- ◆ Sewing needle and thread to match spruce yarn
- ◆ Low-temperature glue gun

Cutting & Stitching
1. Cut plastic canvas according to graphs (pages 130 and 131). Cut one 39-hole x 23-hole piece for box bottom.

2. With spruce, Continental Stitch box bottom. Following graphs, Continental Stitch back-ground on band pieces with Aran.

3. Work dark spruce French Knots and black pearl cotton Back-stitches on band pieces over com-pleted Continental Stitching.

4. Whipstitch side edges of short band pieces and long band pieces together with Aran; Overcast top and bottom edges with medium coral rose.

5. Stitch remaining pieces follow-

ing graphs, reversing one side before stitching.

6. Using spruce through step 7, Overcast all edges of lid, recipe card lip and lip support. Overcast top edges of sides, front and back.

7. With wrong sides facing in, Whipstitch front, back and sides together, then Whipstitch bottom to front, back and sides.

Final Assembly

1. With sewing needle and thread, stitch back edge of lid to top edge of back loosely enough to easily open and close lid.

2. Using photo as a guide through step 3, slide band up around box; glue in place about ⅜" from bottom of box.

3. Matching bottom edges, glue wrong sides of lip and lip support together. Glue bottom edge of lid to lip and lip support, so lid edge rests on top edge of lip support and recipe card lip sticks up slightly above lid, forming the lip to hold recipe card in place. ♦

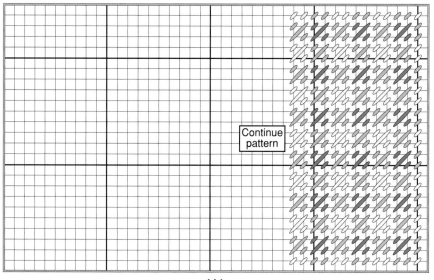

Lid
41 holes x 25 holes
Cut 1

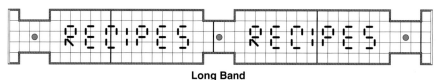

Long Band
41 holes x 5 holes
Cut 2

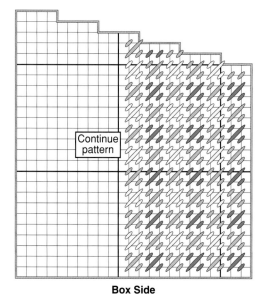

Box Side
23 holes x 25 holes
Cut 2, reverse 1

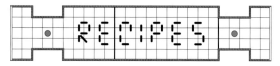

Short Band
25 holes x 5 holes
Cut 2

COLOR KEY	
Worsted Weight Yarn	**Yards**
☐ Aran #313	27
■ Dark spruce #361	38
☐ Spruce #362	47
Uncoded areas on band pieces are Aran #313 Continental Stitches	
╱ Medium coral rose #350 Overcasting	6
● Dark spruce #361 French Knot	
#3 Pearl Cotton	
╱ Black #310 Backstitch	5
Color numbers given are for Red Heart Super Saver worsted weight yarn Art. E301 and DMC #3 Pearl Cotton.	

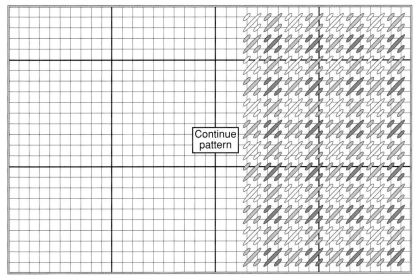

Box Back
39 holes x 25 holes
Cut 1

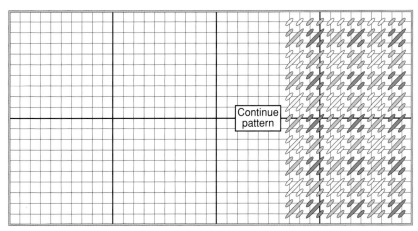

Box Front
39 holes x 20 holes
Cut 1

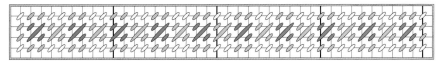

Recipe Card Lip
41 holes x 5 holes
Cut 1

Recipe Card Lip Support
40 holes x 2 holes
Cut 1

Garden Fridgies

Designs by Mary Cosgrove

Stitch up a bushel of cheery and colorful fruits and vegetables
to tack notes and your shopping list to your refrigerator!

Skill Level

Beginner

Materials

◆ ½ sheet Uniek Quick-Count 7-count plastic canvas

◆ Uniek Needloft plastic canvas yarn as listed in color key

◆ #16 tapestry needle

◆ 5 (½") magnet strips

◆ Hot-glue gun

Instructions

1. Cut plastic canvas according to graphs.

2. Stitch pieces, following graphs. Continental Stitch uncoded area on carrot with bright orange, on corn with lemon, on broccoli with fern, on strawberry with red and on watermelon with watermelon following graphs. Overcast pieces following graphs.

3. When background stitching is completed, work embroidery on all pieces, stitching French Knots on broccoli before working holly Straight Stitches.

4. Glue one magnet strip to back of each piece. ◆

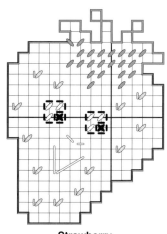

Strawberry
15 holes x 20 holes
Cut 1

COLOR KEY
BROCCOLI

Plastic Canvas Yarn	Yards
■ Black #00	1
■ Holly #27	3
□ White #41	½
Uncoded area is fern #23 Continental Stitches	2
⁄ Fern #23 Overcasting	
⁄ Black #00 Backstitch	
⁄ Holly #27 Staight Stitch	
⁄ White #41 Backstitch and Straight Stitch	
○ Bright green #61 French Knot	

Color numbers given are for Uniek Needloft plastic canvas yarn.

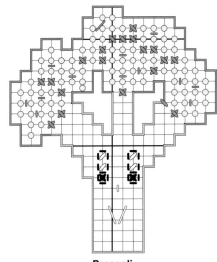

Broccoli
20 holes x 23 holes
Cut 1

COLOR KEY
WATERMELON

Plastic Canvas Yarn	Yards
■ Black #00	1
□ Baby green #26	1
■ Holly #27	2
□ White #41	2
Uncoded area is watermelon #55 Continental Stitches	2
⁄ Watermelon #55 Overcasting	
⁄ Black #00 Backstitch	
⁄ Holly #27 Backstitch	
⁄ White #41 Straight Stitch	

Color numbers given are for Uniek Needloft plastic canvas yarn.

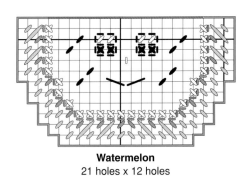

Watermelon
21 holes x 12 holes
Cut 1

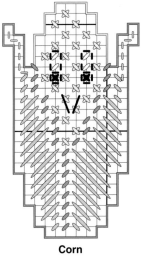

Corn
13 holes x 22 holes
Cut 1

COLOR KEY
CORN

Plastic Canvas Yarn	Yards
■ Black #00	1
□ Fern #23	2
■ Holly #27	2
□ White #41	⅓
□ Yellow #57	1
Uncoded areas are lemon #20 Continental Stitches	1
⁄ Black #00 Backstitch	
⁄ Fern #23 Backstitch	

Color numbers given are for Uniek Needloft plastic canvas yarn.

COLOR KEY
STRAWBERRY

Plastic Canvas Yarn	Yards
■ Black #00	½
□ Lime #22	1
■ Christmas green #28	1
□ White #41	½
Uncoded area is red #01 Continental Stitches	3
⁄ Red #01 Overcasting	
⁄ Black #00 Backstitch	
⁄ Lime #22 Backstitch	
⁄ White #41 Backstitch	

Color numbers given are for Uniek Needloft plastic cavas yarn.

COLOR KEY
CARROT

Plastic Canvas Yarn	Yards
■ Black #00	½
□ Fern #23	1
■ Christmas green #28	1
□ White #41	⅓
Uncoded area is bright orange #58 Continental Stitches	2
⁄ Bright orange #58 Overcasting	
⁄ Black #00 Backstitch	

Color numbers given are for Uniek Needloft plastic canvas yarn.

Carrot
22 holes x 22 holes
Cut 1

Fiesta **Table Set**

Designs by Niki Russos-Atkinson

Serve up a feisty dinner of hot Mexican food on this colorful table set
including a place mat, napkin ring and coaster! Your family will love it!

Skill Level

Beginner

Materials

◆ 2 (12" x 18") sheets Darice
  Super Soft 7-count plastic canvas

◆ 1 sheet regular plastic canvas

◆ Darice Nylon Plus plastic canvas
  yarn as listed in color key

◆ 6-strand embroidery floss
  as listed in color key

Instructions

1. Cut one napkin ring, one napkin
ring pepper and two coasters from
regular plastic canvas according to
graphs (right and page 136). Do

at least two lengths of the same color together.

4. For each two lengths of matching colors, hold four ends together and make one knot close to canvas edge.

5. When all fringe is attached and knotted, smooth out yarn and trim ends evenly.

6. Stitch napkin ring pieces and one coaster following graphs.

Work Backstitches with 6 strands black embroidery floss when background stitching is completed.

7. Place unstitched coaster on wrong side of stitched coaster and Whipstitch together with Christmas green.

8. Using white throughout, Whipstitch short ends of napkin ring to pepper sides from dot to dot. Overcast all remaining edges. ◆

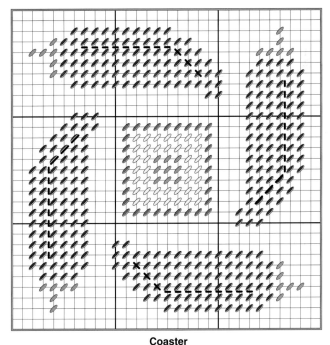

Coaster
30 holes x 30 holes
Cut 2, stitch 1

not cut soft plastic canvas. One coaster piece and one sheet of soft plastic canvas will remain unstitched.

2. Stitch place mat on one sheet soft plastic canvas following graph (page 136). With Christmas green, Whipstitch unstitched sheet of soft plastic to wrong side of stitched place mat along long edges.

3. For fringe, thread 6" lengths of yarn through holes indicated along both short edges of place mat, noting there will always be

COLOR KEY	
COASTER	
Plastic Canvas Yarn	**Yards**
■ Christmas red #19	7
■ Purple #21	1
☐ Yellow #26	1
■ Christmas green #58	2
Uncoded areas are white	
#01 Continental Stitches	8
6-Strand Embroidery Floss	
╱ Black Backstitch	1
Color numbers given are for Darice Nylon Plus yarn.	

COLOR KEY
NAPKIN RING

Plastic Canvas Yarn	Yards
■ Christmas red #19	2
■ Christmas green #58	3
⁄ White #01 Overcasting and Whipstitching	2
6-Strand Embroidery Floss	
⁄ Black Backstitch	1

Color numbers given are for Darice Nylon Plus yarn.

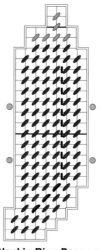

Napkin Ring Pepper
8 holes x 22 holes
Cut 1

Continue pattern

COLOR KEY
PLACE MAT

Plastic Canvas Yarn	Yards
☐ White #01	33
■ Christmas red #19	24
▥ Purple #21	29
☐ Yellow #26	27
▨ Christmas green #58	25
○ Attach white #01 fringe	
● Attach Christmas red #19 fringe	
● Attach purple #21 fringe	
○ Attach yellow #26 fringe	
◉ Attach Christmas green #58 fringe	

Color numbers given are for Darice Nylon Plus yarn.

Continue pattern

Napkin Ring
6 holes x 34 holes
Cut 1

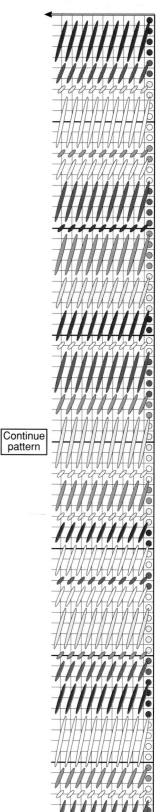

Place Mat
120 holes x 80 holes
Stitch 1

Birdhouse Coaster Set

Design by Linda Wyszynski

Delight guests by using this set of lovely coasters. The set makes a thoughtful hostess gift, too.

Skill Level

Intermediate

Materials

- ◆ *3 sheets 10-count plastic canvas*
- ◆ *DMC #3 pearl cotton as listed in color key*
- ◆ *DMC 6-strand embroidery floss as listed in color key*
- ◆ *#20 tapestry needle*

Instructions

1. Cut plastic canvas according to graphs (right and page 138). Four coasters, one front, one back and two sides will be used for lining and will remain unstitched.

2. Cut two 39-hole x 10-hole pieces for holder bottom. Holder bottom pieces will remain unstitched.

3. Following graph, stitch holder front, using double strand very light old gold for roof and double strand light beige brown for back-

Coaster
47 holes x 41 holes
Cut 8, stitch 4

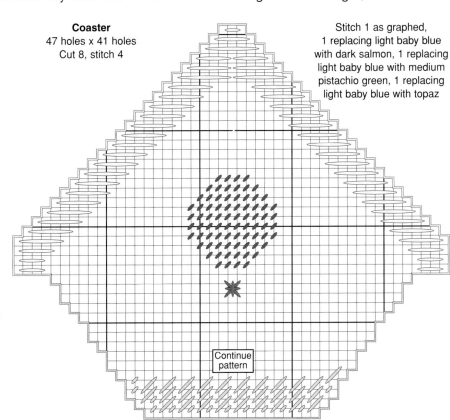

Stitch 1 as graphed,
1 replacing light baby blue
with dark salmon, 1 replacing
light baby blue with medium
pistachio green, 1 replacing
light baby blue with topaz

Continue
pattern

ground. When background stitching is completed, stitch embroidery with 6 strands floss, working French Knots last.

4. Using double strand light baby blue, stitch one back and two sides following graphs.

5. Stitch four coasters following graph, working one house with light baby blue as graphed, one with dark salmon, one with medium pistachio green and one with topaz. Work roofs with double strand very light old gold.

6. Whipstitch roof edges of front and unstitched front lining together with one strand very light old gold.

7. Using one strand light baby blue throughout, Whipstitch top edges of back and unstitched back lining together. Repeat with side pieces. Working through all four thicknesses, Whipstitch sides to back; place bottom pieces together and Whipstitch to sides and back.

8. Using one strand light beige brown and working through all four thicknesses, Whipstitch side and bottom edges of holder front to holder sides and bottom.

9. Whipstitch one unstitched lining piece to back of each coaster with adjacent colors. ◆

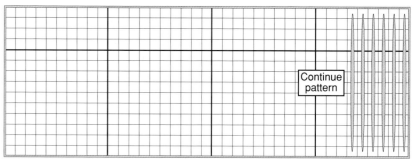

Coaster Holder Back
39 holes x 14 holes
Cut 2, stitch 1

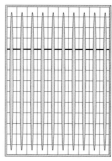

Coaster Holder Side
10 holes x 14 holes
Cut 4, stitch 2

Coaster Holder Front
47 holes x 41 holes
Cut 2, stitch 1

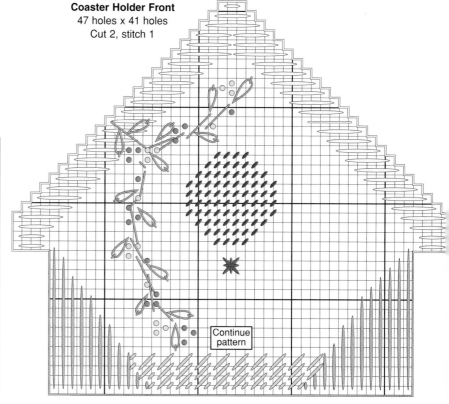

COLOR KEY	
#3 Pearl Cotton	**Yards**
Medium pistachio green #320	11
☐ Very light old gold #677	23
Topaz #725	11
■ Dark navy blue #823	6
■ Very dark beige brown #838	2
▨ Light beige brown #841	5
▨ Light baby blue #3325	33
Dark salmon #3328	11
6-Strand Embroidery Floss	
╱ Medium pistachio green #320 Straight Stitch	1
⬭ Medium pistachio green #320 Lazy Daisy	
○ Topaz #725 French Knot	1
● Dark salmon #3328 French Knot	1
Color numbers given are for DMC #3 pearl cotton and 6-strand embroidery floss.	

Baby Love

Delight the parents-to-be with a variety of pretty and practical gifts for welcoming their new baby! This collection of gifts includes ideas for newborns through toddlers that are sure to please Mom, Dad and the little one!

Lucky Duck **Gift Caddy**

Design by Janelle Giese • Shown on page 139

Here's a terrific gift for a baby shower! Fill this darling little ducky with an assortment of baby supplies as a treat for the expectant mommy.

Skill Level

Advanced

Materials

◆ 1 artist-size sheet 7-count plastic canvas

◆ Uniek Needloft plastic canvas yarn as listed in color key

◆ Kreinik ⅛" Ribbon as listed in color key

◆ DMC #3 pearl cotton as listed in color key

◆ DMC 6-strand embroidery floss as listed in color key

◆ #16 tapestry needle

◆ 1 yard 1"-wide yellow satin ribbon

◆ Sewing needle and yellow sewing thread

◆ Trial-size baby products

◆ Excelsior or basket/gift filler as desired

Cutting & Stitching

1. Cut plastic canvas according to graphs (pages 140—142). Base will remain unstitched.

2. Stitch remaining pieces following graphs, leaving blue line on gusset unstitched at this time.

3. Over straw Continental Stitches, Cross Stitch cheeks with 1 strand embroidery floss. Work white yarn Straight Stitch for highlight on eyes and black pearl cotton Backstitches for outlining around heart, wings and eyes.

4. With tangerine, Overcast bill

around side and bottom edges from dot to dot; Whipstitch dart together at center top. With straw, Overcast inside edges on gusset.

Assembly

1. Use photo as a guide throughout assembly. Using straw through step 4 and beginning at bottom front edge, Whipstitch gusset sides to front and back until one bar above unstitched blue line on gusset. *Note: It will be necessary to ease gusset to front and back around curves throughout Whipstitching.*

2. With tangerine, Whipstitch unstitched edges of duck bill to gusset, front and back where indicated along blue lines, attaching bill to front and back over straw Continental Stitches. Continue Whipstitching gusset to front and back up to tail edge.

3. Following Fig. 1, Whipstitch top edge of tail to tail end of gusset, then Whipstitch tail sides to front and back. Whipstitch remaining back edges of front and back together, stopping just before bottom edge is reached.

4. Whipstitch unstitched base to gusset, front and back, easing around curves.

5. Tie ribbon in a bow around neck, trimming edges as desired. Tack ribbon in place with sewing needle and yellow sewing thread.

6. Fill duck with excelsior and trial-size baby products. ◆

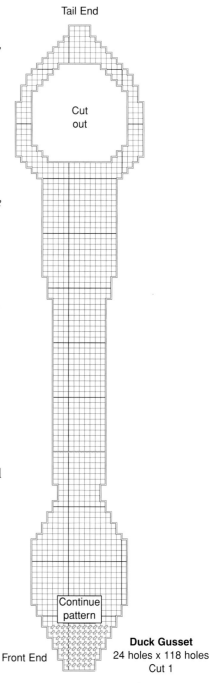

Tail End

Cut out

Front End

Continue pattern

Duck Gusset
24 holes x 118 holes
Cut 1

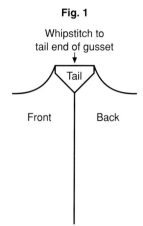

Fig. 1

Whipstitch to
tail end of gusset

Tail

Front   Back

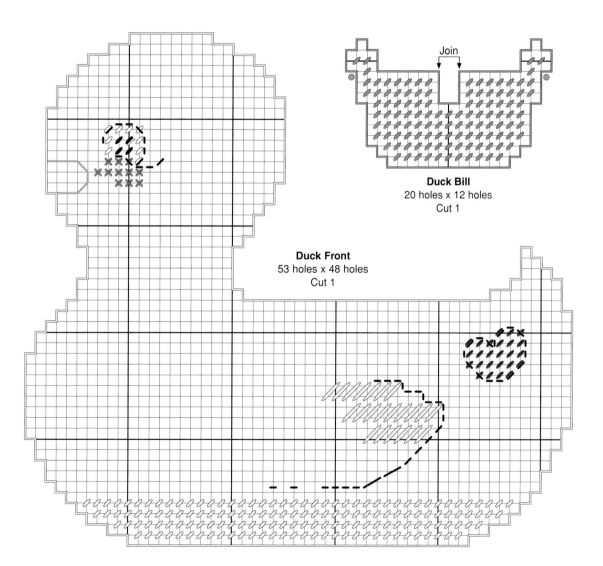

Duck Bill
20 holes x 12 holes
Cut 1

Join

Duck Front
53 holes x 48 holes
Cut 1

COLOR KEY

Plastic Canvas Yarn	Yards
■ Black #00	1
▨ Tangerine #11	4
▢ Straw #19	82
▢ White #41	1
⁄ White #41 Straight Stitch	
⅛" Ribbon	
■ Red #003	1
#3 Pearl Cotton	
⁄ Black #310 Backstitch	2
6-Strand Embroidery Floss	
✖ Ultra dark dusty rose	1
#3350 Cross Stitch	
⁄ Attach duck bill	

Color numbers given are for Uniek Needloft plastic canvas yarn, Kreinik ⅛" Ribbon and DMC #3 pearl cotton and 6-strand embroidery floss.

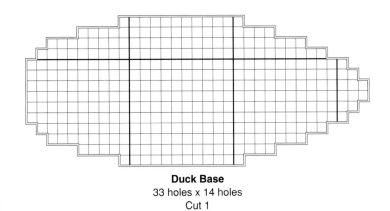

Duck Base
33 holes x 14 holes
Cut 1
Do not stitch

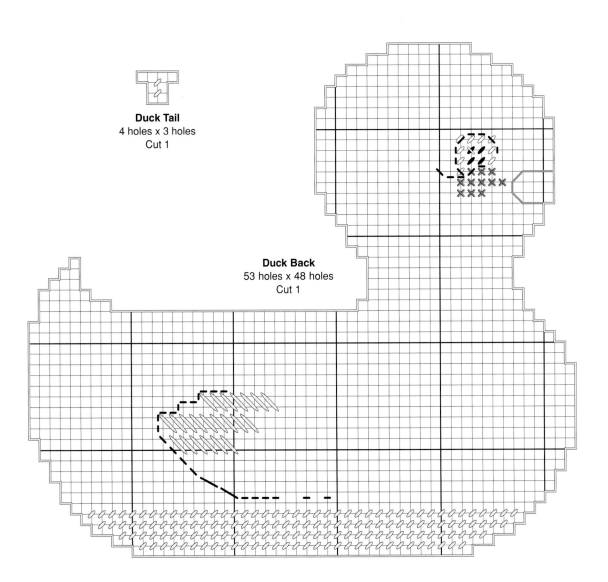

Duck Tail
4 holes x 3 holes
Cut 1

Duck Back
53 holes x 48 holes
Cut 1

Teddy Bear
Picnic

Design by Janelle Giese

Start saving now for a rainy day with this delightful musical bank! As your little ones watch the bank fill up, they'll look forward to that rainy day!

Skill Level
Advanced

Materials
◆ 1 artist-size sheet Darice Ultra Stiff 7-count plastic canvas

◆ Uniek Needloft plastic canvas yarn as listed in color key

◆ Kreinik ⅛" Ribbon as listed in color key

◆ DMC #5 pearl cotton as listed in color key

◆ #16 tapestry needle

◆ Teddy Bear Picnic electronic music bank #P10693-43 by Darice

◆ Heavy sewing thread

◆ Thick white glue

Instructions
1. Cut plastic canvas according to graphs (pages 144 and 145). Cut one 29-hole x 12-hole piece for bank base, two 26-hole x 4-hole pieces for lip long sides and two 9-hole x 4-hole pieces for lip short sides. Bank front, base and lip pieces will remain unstitched.

2. Stitch picnic scene following graph, working uncoded tree and bush areas with moss Continental Stitches and uncoded areas on bears with beige Continental Stitches.

3. When background stitching is completed, work embroidery with black pearl cotton. Overcast inside and outside edges following graphs, leaving bottom and side edges from dot to dot unstitched at this time.

4. Using eggshell through step 7, stitch bank sides and back following graphs. Overcast top edges of sides, back and front.

5. Whipstitch lip pieces together, forming a rectangle. Place top edges of lip pieces against lid where indicated on graph and attach to lid while working Slanted Gobelin Stitches; Overcast inside and outside edges of lid.

6. Whipstitch sides to back and unstitched front. Whipstitch base to back and sides. Do not stitch base to front at this time.

7. Center picnic scene on bank front, making sure bottom edges are even. With lavender, Overcast side and bottom edges of scene from dot to dot, Whipstitching scene to front and base through all thicknesses while Overcasting.

8. With heavy sewing thread, tack picnic scene to top part of box front in at least two places.

9. Glue music bank into lid opening. Allow to dry. Place lid on completed bank. ◆

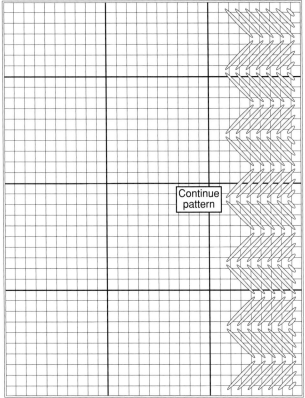

Bank Front & Back
29 holes x 37 holes
Cut 2
Stitch back only

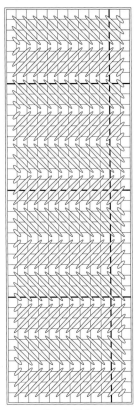

Bank Side
12 holes x 37 holes
Cut 2

COLOR KEY	
Plastic Canvas Yarn	**Yards**
■ Lavender #05	2
■ Cinnamon #14	3
■ Christmas green #28	11
■ Cerulean #34	1
□ Baby blue #36	1
□ Eggshell #39	38
□ White #41	1
■ Camel #43	2
■ Lilac #45	3
■ Peach #47	1
Uncoded areas on tree and bushes are moss #25 Continental Stitches	8
Uncoded areas on bears are beige #40 Continental Stitches	3
⅛" Ribbon	
■ Star mauve #093	1
□ Sunlight #9100	2
□ Blossom #9200	2
#5 Pearl Cotton	
╱ Black #310 Backstitch and Straight Stitch	6
╱ Attach lip pieces	
Color numbers given are for Uniek Needloft plastic canvas yarn, Kreinik ⅛" Ribbon and DMC #5 pearl cotton.	

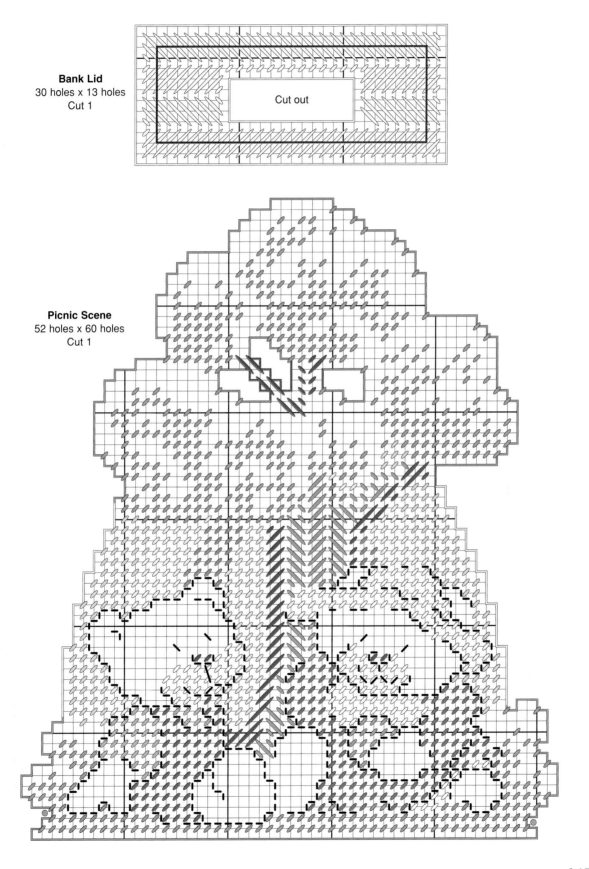

Bank Lid
30 holes x 13 holes
Cut 1

Cut out

Picnic Scene
52 holes x 60 holes
Cut 1

Baby's First Frame

Design by Kimberly A. Suber

Stitch this adorable frame as a special gift for Mom, Dad, Grandma, Grandpa or just about any doting family member!

Skill Level
Beginner

Materials
- 1 sheet 7-count plastic canvas
- Worsted weight yarn as listed in color key
- #16 tapestry needle
- Hot-glue gun

Instructions
1. Cut plastic canvas according to graphs (below and page 147). Cut one 17-hole x 27-hole piece for frame stand. Frame back and stand will remain unstitched.

2. Stitch pieces following graphs, reversing one duck before stitching. Work uncoded areas on baby blocks with ecru. Work black French Knots on ducks when background stitching is completed.

3. Overcast duck bills with orange and remaining edges with yellow. Overcast heart with bright pink and inside edges of frame front with fuchsia. Overcast baby blocks following graphs.

4. With white, Whipstitch top edge of stand to frame back where indicated on graph with blue line. Whipstitch wrong sides of frame front and back together with fuchsia.

5. Using photo as a guide throughout, glue baby blocks to top of frame front so they spell "BABY." Making sure bottom edges are even, glue ducks to bottom corners, then glue heart between ducks. ◆

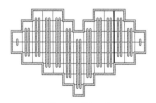

Frame Heart
13 holes x 8 holes
Cut 1

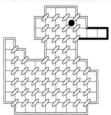

Frame Duck
10 holes x 10 holes
Cut 2, reverse 1

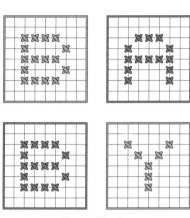

Frame Blocks
8 holes x 8 holes
Cut 1 each

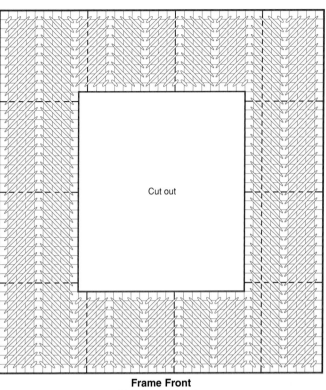

Cut out

Frame Front
37 holes x 40 holes
Cut 1

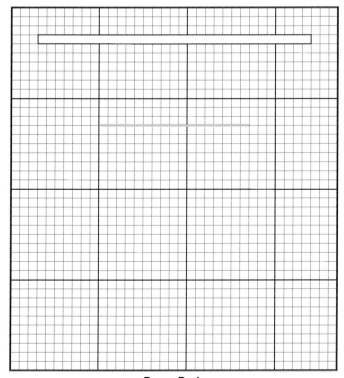

Frame Back
37 holes x 40 holes
Cut 1

COLOR KEY	
Worsted Weight Yarn	**Yards**
☐ White	7
▨ Bright pink	2
☐ Yellow	2
▨ Tangerine	1
■ Royal	1
▨ Purple	1
▨ Green	1
Uncoded areas are ecru	
Continental Stitches	2
╱ Fuchsia Overcasting	
and Whipstitching	3
╱ Orange Overcasting	1
● Black French Knot	1

Baby's First Christmas Ornament

Design by Vicki Blizzard

Frame your precious little one in one of these perfectly pretty baby rattle ornaments!
Be sure to tuck it away in his or her keepsake chest!

Skill Level
Beginner

Materials
Each Rattle

- ¼ sheet Uniek Quick-Count clear 7-count plastic canvas
- ¼ sheet Uniek Quick-Count pastel pink or pastel blue 7-count plastic canvas
- Spinrite plastic canvas yarn as listed in color key
- DMC #3 pearl cotton as listed in color key
- #16 tapestry needle
- 6 (4mm) pink Austrian glass rhinestones from National Artcraft
- 9" ¼"-wide white picot-edge satin ribbon
- 12" fine white cord
- Hot-glue gun

Project Notes

If using pastel pink plastic canvas for rattle back, use cherry blossom yarn and very light carnation pearl cotton.

If using pastel blue plastic canvas for rattle back, use sky yarn and light blue pearl cotton.

White and seafoam yarn are used for both rattles.

Instructions

1. Cut rattle front and leaves from

clear plastic canvas; cut rattle back from pastel pink or pastel blue plastic canvas according to graphs. Rattle back will remain unstitched.

2. Stitch front and leaves following graphs. Work Straight Stitches on leaves over completed background stitching.

3. From clear plastic canvas, cut one year plate 5 holes high and as wide as necessary to fit desired year (see numbers), leaving one row of Continental Stitches around year and between numbers. *Note: Sample used 9-hole x 5-hole piece.*

4. Continental Stitch year plate with white yarn. Overcast edges with cherry blossom or sky. With very light carnation or light blue pearl cotton, Backstitch year over completed background stitching.

5. Using cherry blossom or sky throughout, Overcast edges of photo opening on rattle front. Whipstitch front to unstitched back around outside edges and around inside hole on rattle bottom.

6. Using photo as a guide throughout, glue three rhinestones to each leaf. Glue year plate and leaves to rattle front. Tie ribbon in a bow; trim ends. Glue bow to handle.

7. For hanger, attach white cord to rattle where indicated on graph with a Lark's Head Knot (Fig. 1). Tie cord ends together in a knot to form a loop for hanging. ◆

COLOR KEY

Plastic Canvas Yarn	Yards
□ White #0001	3
■ Sky #0004 or cherry blossom #0010	5
■ Seafoam #0013	1
╱ Seafoam #0013 Straight Stitch	
#3 Pearl Cotton	
╱ Light blue #813 or very light carnation #894 Backstitch	½
● Attach white cord	

Color numbers given are for Spinrite plastic canvas yarn and DMC #3 pearl cotton.

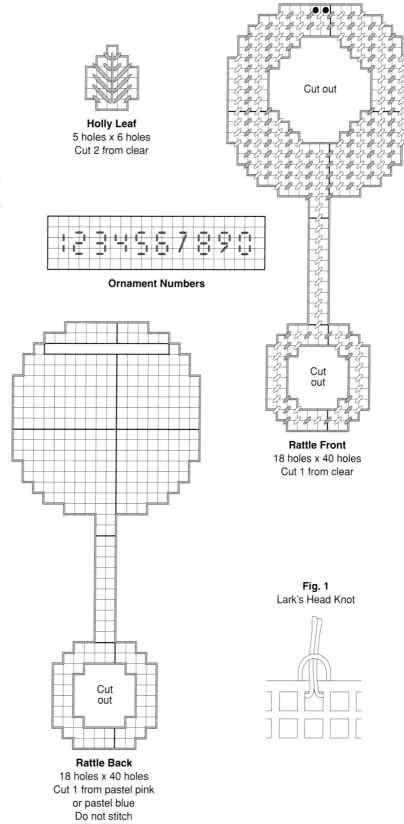

Holly Leaf
5 holes x 6 holes
Cut 2 from clear

Ornament Numbers

Rattle Front
18 holes x 40 holes
Cut 1 from clear

Fig. 1
Lark's Head Knot

Rattle Back
18 holes x 40 holes
Cut 1 from pastel pink or pastel blue
Do not stitch

Bright Checks Diaper Dispenser

Design by Joan Green

Every parent knows the importance of having lots of diapers close at hand!
This cheery diaper dispenser will add a splash of color and cheer to diapering Baby.

Skill Level
Beginner

Materials
- 2 artist-size sheets 5-count plastic canvas
- Spinrite Bernat Berella "4" worsted weight yarn as listed in color key
- #16 tapestry needle
- 30" 1"-wide white satin ribbon
- 5⅞" x 8⅞" piece white cardboard
- Hot-glue gun

Project Notes
Use a double strand of yarn for all stitching.

For stitching with white yarn, cut yarn into 4-yard lengths, then double over to create a 2-yard double strand.

For stitching with colored yarn, cut yarn into 6-yard lengths, then double over to create a 3-yard double strand.

Instructions
1. Cut plastic canvas according to graphs (pages 151 and 152). Back and bottom will remain unstitched.

2. Following graphs and Project Notes for remaining pieces, Continental Stitch dividing lines with white first. Fill in squares with Scotch Stitches, working each color back and forth diagonally.

3. Using white through step 4, Overcast bottom edges of front. Whipstitch front, back and sides together, making sure top edge on front is even with top edges on sides.

4. Whipstitch top to front, back and sides; Whipstitch bottom to back and sides. Overcast remaining edges on dispenser.

5. Cut white satin ribbon in half. Place ribbon lengths together and tie in a bow, trimming ends as desired. Glue bow to dispenser front where indicated on graph.

6. Place cardboard in dispenser for bottom lining. Place diapers in dispenser through hole in back. ◆

COLOR KEY	
Worsted Weight Yarn	**Yards**
▨ Aquamarine #8702	42
▨ Watermelon #8703	42
▧ Tangelo #8704	42
▨ Mega magenta #8707	42
▨ Pretty purple #8708	42
▢ White #8942	140
○ Attach ribbon bow	

Color numbers given are for Spinrite Bernat Berella "4" worsted weight yarn.

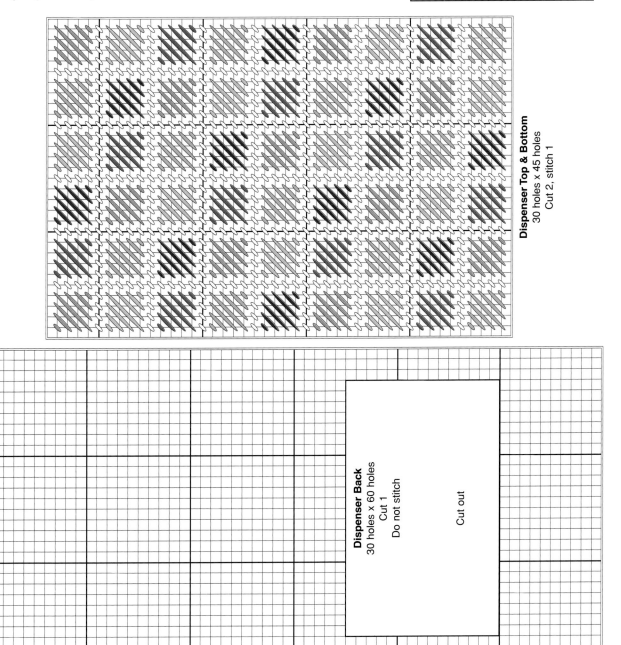

Dispenser Top & Bottom
30 holes x 45 holes
Cut 2, stitch 1

Dispenser Back
30 holes x 60 holes
Cut 1
Do not stitch

Cut out

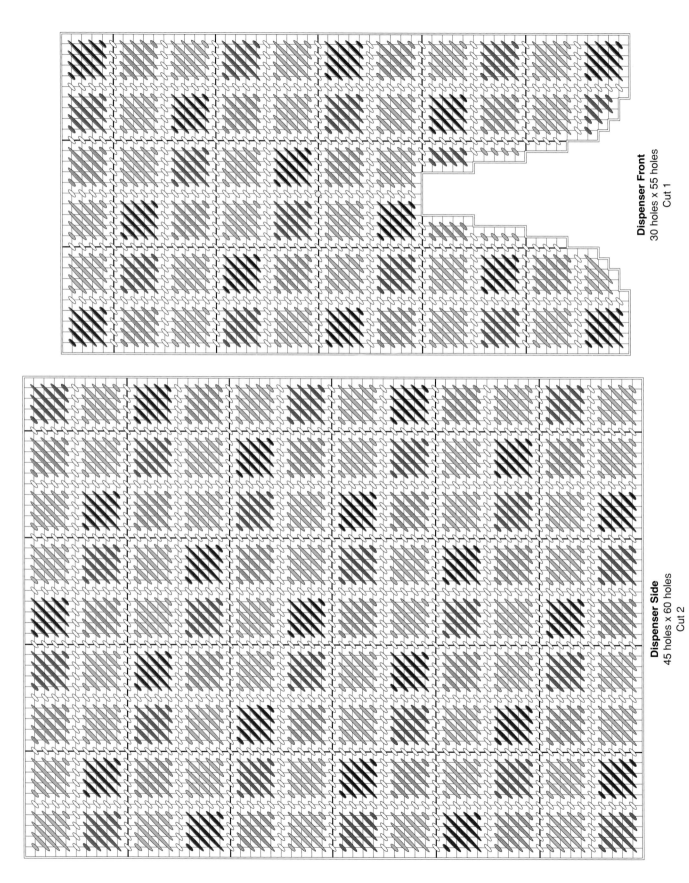

Dispenser Front
30 holes x 55 holes
Cut 1

Dispenser Side
45 holes x 60 holes
Cut 2

Grandma's Pride & Joy

Design by Mary T. Cosgrove

It won't take Grandma much time at all to fill this charming
photo album with dozens of pictures of her newest pride and joy!

Skill Level

Beginner

Materials

- ◆ *2 sheets Uniek Quick-Count 7-count plastic canvas*
- ◆ *Uniek Needloft plastic canvas yarn as listed in color key*
- ◆ *#16 tapestry needle*
- ◆ *3-hole photo album inserts*
- ◆ *1 yard ¼"-wide yellow satin ribbon*

Instructions

1. Cut front cover, back cover, left front and spine from plastic canvas according to graphs (pages 154–156).

2. Stitch pieces following graphs. Overcast inside edges on back and left front with baby green.

3. Using baby green throughout, Overcast top and bottom edges of all pieces and outside edges of front and back covers.

4. Whipstitch spine to remaining edge of back cover and to edge indicated on left front; Whipstitch remaining edges of left front and front cover together.

5. Place three-hole photo album inserts inside album and align holes with front and back covers. Thread ribbon from front to back through center hole (step A), leaving an 8" tail on front.

6. Bring ribbon down to bottom hole and thread from back to front (step B). Bring ribbon back up to center hole and thread from front to back (step C).

7. Bring ribbon up to top hole and thread from back to front (step D). Bring ribbon down to ribbons at center hole and slide under ribbon from step C; do not thread ribbon through hole.

8. Tie ends in a knot. Make sure tails are even, then tie in a bow on front. ◆

Whipstitch this edge to spine →

COLOR KEY

Plastic Canvas Yarn	Yards
■ Pink #07	4
□ Lemon #20	8
■ Baby green #26	35
□ White #41	84
Color numbers given are for Uniek Needloft plastic canvas yarn.	

Left Front
7 holes x 75 holes
Cut 1

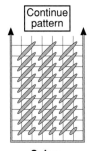

Continue pattern

Spine
7 holes x 75 holes
Cut 1

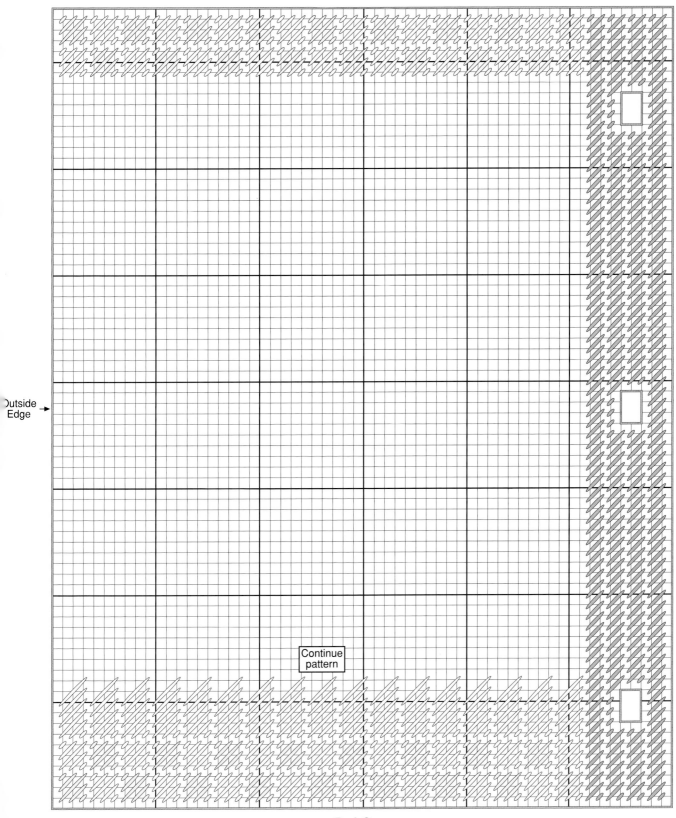

Outside Edge →

Continue pattern

Back Cover
60 holes x 75 holes
Cut 1

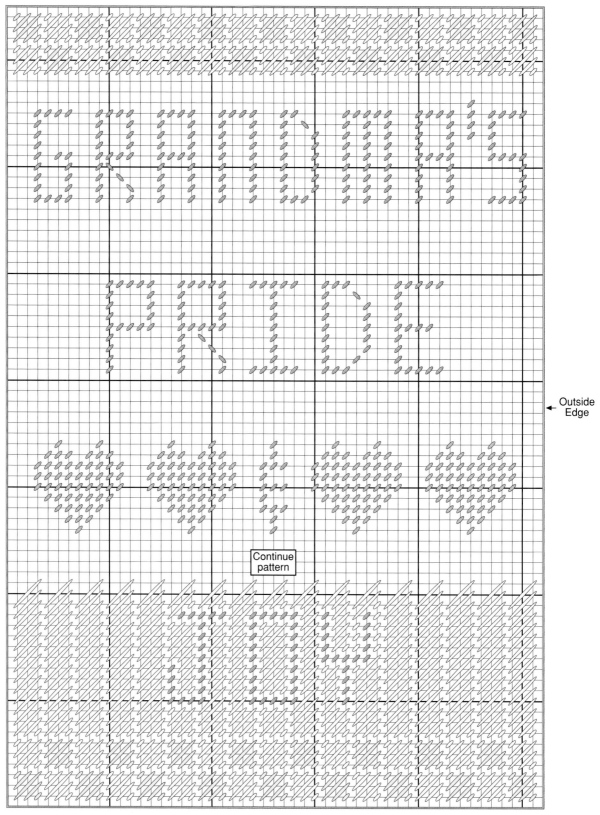

Front Cover
52 holes x 75 holes
Cut 1

Gift Bags for All

Now that you've found the perfect gift for your special occasion, why not give two gifts in one by giving your gift in a lovely, hand-stitched bag or box? Your friends and family will surely love these gifts that keep on giving!

Sunny Sunflower Tote

Design by Kimberly A. Suber • Shown on page 156

This cheery tote is ideal for many gift-giving occasions,
from carrying a housewarming surprise to a special birthday gift!

Skill Level

Beginner

Materials

◆ *1 regular sheet 7-count plastic canvas*

◆ *12" x 18" sheet 7-count plastic canvas*

◆ *Worsted weight yarn as listed in color key*

◆ *#16 tapestry needle*

◆ *4 (⅞") yellow buttons*

◆ *¾" blue button*

◆ *7" ⅛"-wide yellow satin ribbon*

◆ *Miniature chenille bee*

◆ *Miniature chenille ladybug*

◆ *Hot-glue gun*

Instructions

1. Cut plastic canvas according to graphs. Cut one 55-hole x 19-hole piece for tote bottom. Tote bottom will remain unstitched.

2. Stitch pieces following graphs. Overcast sunflower center with brown, then work French Knots. Work Straight Stitches on leaves and petals when background stitching is completed.

3. Overcast stem, leaves, petals and flowerpot with adjacent colors. With blue yarn, sew yellow buttons to four corners of tote front as in photo.

4. Using blue throughout, Overcast top edges of tote front, back and sides and all edges of handles. Whipstitch front and back to sides, then Whipstitch front, back and sides to unstitched bottom.

5. Using photo as a guide through step 8, glue wrong side of one set of petals to right side of second set, evenly spacing top petals between bottom petals. Glue flower center to center of top petals.

6. Glue stem to back of pot and sunflower; glue leaves to stem. Making sure bottom edges are even, center and glue assembled flower and pot to tote front.

7. Glue bee to sunflower center, and ladybug to one leaf. Thread yellow ribbon from front to back through holes on blue button; tie ribbon in a bow. Glue button to center front of pot. If desired, glue ribbon ends to pot.

8. Glue one handle to tote front, placing right side of handle ends on wrong side of tote front. Repeat with remaining handle and tote back. ◆

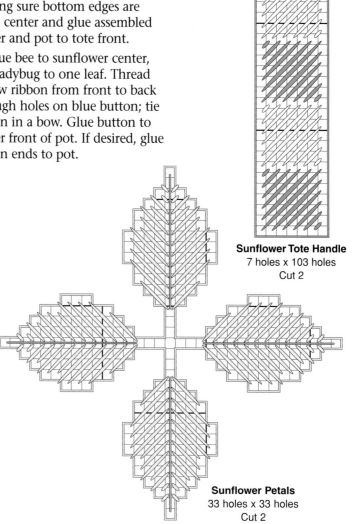

Continue pattern

Sunflower Tote Handle
7 holes x 103 holes
Cut 2

Sunflower Petals
33 holes x 33 holes
Cut 2

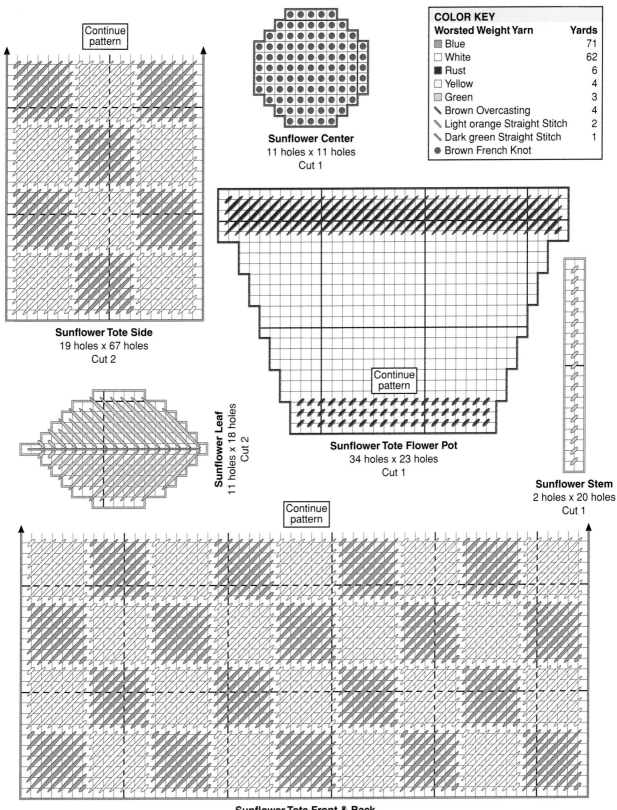

COLOR KEY

Worsted Weight Yarn	Yards
▨ Blue	71
☐ White	62
■ Rust	6
☐ Yellow	4
▨ Green	3
╲ Brown Overcasting	4
╲ Light orange Straight Stitch	2
╲ Dark green Straight Stitch	1
● Brown French Knot	

Continue pattern

Sunflower Center
11 holes x 11 holes
Cut 1

Sunflower Tote Side
19 holes x 67 holes
Cut 2

Sunflower Leaf
11 holes x 18 holes
Cut 2

Continue pattern

Sunflower Tote Flower Pot
34 holes x 23 holes
Cut 1

Sunflower Stem
2 holes x 20 holes
Cut 1

Continue pattern

Sunflower Tote Front & Back
55 holes x 67 holes
Cut 2

Primary Colors Gift Box

Design by Ronda Bryce

Kids will especially love this bright and bold gift box decorated with lots of colors and crayons, too!

Skill Level

Beginner

Materials

- *2 sheets 7-count plastic canvas*
- *Spinrite plastic canvas yarn as listed in color key*
- *#16 tapestry needle*
- *5 (12mm x 10mm) heart pony beads in colors to match yarn*
- *4 crayons: red, orange, yellow and green*
- *Sewing needle and black sewing thread*

Instructions

1. Cut plastic canvas according to graphs. Cut one 29-hole square for box bottom. Box bottom will remain unstitched.

2. Stitch pieces following graphs.

With sewing needle and black thread, attach one bead to center of each side and to center of lid top.

3. Using black through step 6, Overcast bottom edges of lid sides and top edges of box sides.

4. Using two stitches per hole throughout, Whipstitch lid sides together, then Whipstitch lid sides to lid top.

5. Whipstitch box sides together,

placing sides A opposite each other and sides B opposite each other; Whipstitch box sides to box bottom.

6. Using photo as a guide, stitch one crayon to each box corner. ◆

COLOR KEY	
Plastic Canvas Yarn	**Yards**
▦ Lilac #0008	7
■ Scarlet #0022	7
▨ Royal #0026	7
■ Black #0028	35
☐ Daffodil #0029	8
▨ Orange #0030	7
▨ Apple #0041	8
Color numbers given are for Spinrite plastic canvas yarn.	

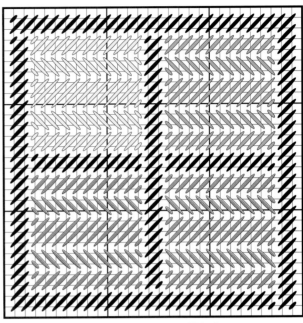

Primary Colors Box Side A
29 holes x 29 holes
Cut 2

Primary Colors Lid Side
31 holes x 3 holes
Cut 4

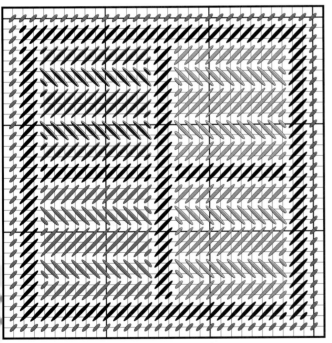

Primary Colors Lid Top
31 holes x 31 holes
Cut 1

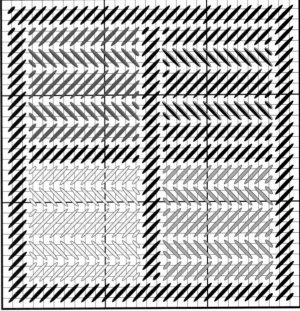

Primary Colors Box Side B
29 holes x 29 holes
Cut 2

Pretty Pastels **Gift Boxes**

Designs by Laura Scott

This pair of pretty gift boxes can be stitched in soft colors as shown
for a bridal or baby shower, or in rich jewel tones for many other occasions.

Skill Level
Beginner

CHECKERED BOX

Materials
◆ 1 sheet clear stiff
   7-count plastic canvas

◆ ½ sheet pink regular
   7-count plastic canvas

◆ Uniek Needloft plastic canvas
   yarn as listed in color key

◆ 10" ⅛"-wide pink picot-edge
   satin ribbon

◆ Hot-glue gun

Instructions
1. Cut lid pieces from clear stiff
plastic canvas according to graphs
(page 163).

2. From pink plastic canvas, cut
one 36-hole x 26-hole piece for
box bottom, two 26-hole x 11-
hole pieces for box short sides
and two 36-hole x 11-hole pieces
for box long sides. Box pieces will
remain unstitched.

3. Stitch lid pieces following graphs.

4. Using baby pink through step
5, Whipstitch lid short sides to lid
long sides, then Whipstitch lid

sides to lid top. Overcast bottom
edges.

5. For box, Whipstitch short sides
to long sides, then Whipstitch
sides to bottom. Overcast top
edges. Slide lid over box.

6. Tie ribbon in a bow. Glue to
top left corner. Trim ends.

PINK & WHITE BOX
Materials
◆ 1 sheet clear stiff
   7-count plastic canvas

◆ ½ sheet pink regular
   plastic canvas

- Uniek Needloft plastic canvas yarn as listed in color key
- 20" 1⅜"-wide white box-pleated trim
- Hot-glue gun
- 2 (8" x 11") pieces white felt (optional)

Instructions

1. Cut lid, box long sides and box short sides from clear stiff plastic canvas according to graphs (page 164).

2. From pink plastic canvas, cut one 49-hole x 35-hole piece for box bottom. Box bottom will remain unstitched.

3. If lining is desired, cut one piece of felt for box lid and each side and two pieces of felt for box bottom, cutting felt slightly smaller than matching plastic canvas piece.

4. Stitch pieces following graphs.

5. Using baby pink through step 6, Whipstitch short sides to long sides, then Whipstitch sides to bottom. Whipstitch one long side to one long edge of top. Overcast remaining edges of lid and sides.

6. Glue box-pleated trim to wrong side of lid around edge, easing around corners.

7. If lining box with felt, glue felt inside box to lid and sides; glue one piece of felt to both sides of box bottom. ◆

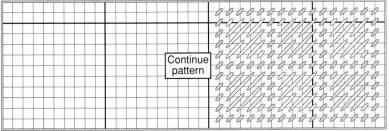

Checkered Box Lid Long Side
37 holes x 12 holes
Cut 2 from clear

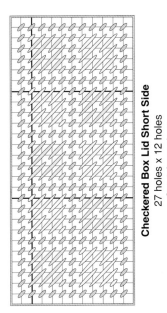

Checkered Box Lid Short Side
27 holes x 12 holes
Cut 2 from clear

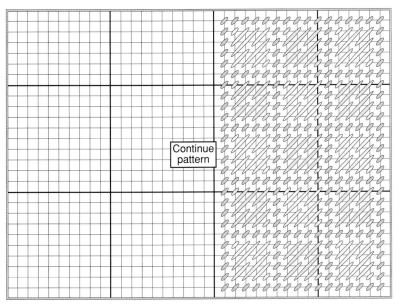

Checkered Box Lid Top
37 holes x 27 holes
Cut 1 from clear

COLOR KEY	
CHECKERED BOX	
Plastic Canvas Yarn	**Yards**
☐ Baby pink #08	25
☐ Baby yellow #21	20
☐ Baby blue #36	20
Color numbers given are for Uniek Needloft plastic canvas yarn.	

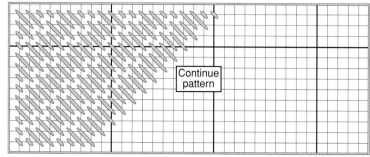

Pink & White Box Short Side
35 holes x 14 holes
Cut 2 from clear

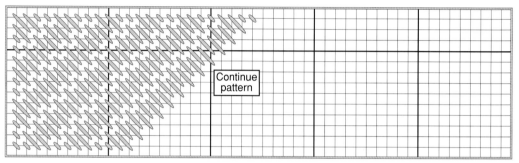

Pink & White Box Long Side
49 holes x 14 holes
Cut 2 from clear

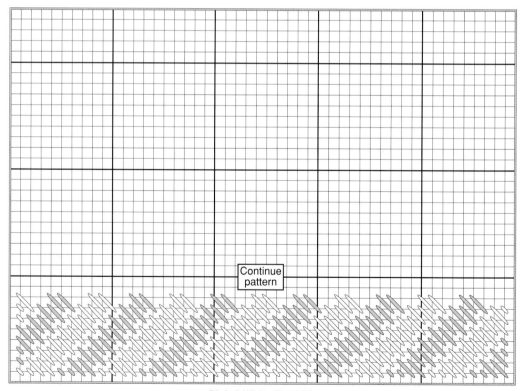

Pink & White Box Lid
49 holes x 35 holes
Cut 1 from clear

A *Starry* Christmas Bag

Design by Celia Lange Designs

Delight a friend or family member by tucking this year's
Christmas gift inside this extra-special holiday gift bag!

Skill Level

Beginner

Materials

- ◆ *2 sheets Darice Ultra Stiff 7-count plastic canvas*
- ◆ *¼ sheet lengthwise 7-count regular plastic canvas*
- ◆ *Red Heart Classic worsted weight yarn Art. E267 as listed in color key*
- ◆ *DMC #3 pearl cotton as listed in color key*
- ◆ *#16 tapestry needle*
- ◆ *Christmas Stitchery buttons by La Mode from Blumenthal Lansing Co.: 2 reindeer #1654 2 Christmas trees #1658 2 Santas #1664 2 angels #1666*
- ◆ *2 Button Crafts 1" wooden star buttons by La Mode from Blumenthal Lansing Co.*
- ◆ *Olde gold #DA176 Americana acrylic paint from DecoArt*
- ◆ *Paintbrush*
- ◆ *2⅜" x 1¼" piece cardboard or heavy white paper*
- ◆ *Hot-glue gun*

Instructions

1. Paint star buttons with olde gold acrylic paint. Allow to dry.

2. Cut plastic canvas according to graphs. Cut one 56-hole x 20-hole piece for bag bottom.

3. Stitch bottom with paddy green Continental Stitches. Stitch remaining pieces following graphs, working uncoded areas with off-white Continental Stitches. When background stitching is completed, embroider words with pearl cotton.

4. Center and stitch stars to front and back with honey gold yarn.

5. With honey gold, Overcast top edges of front, back and sides, then Whipstitch bottom to front, back and sides. Overcast handles with cherry red and paddy green following graph.

6. Overcast inside edges of tags with paddy green. Overcast left sides of tags from dot to dot following graph. With wrong sides facing, Whipstitch remaining edges of tag pieces together with cherry red.

7. Using photo as a guide throughout, glue handles inside basket front and back. Glue Santa, tree and reindeer buttons and sew angel buttons with cherry red to corresponding squares on front and back where indicated on graph.

8. Write name on cardboard and decorate as desired. Place cardboard inside stitched tag. Thread a length of cherry red yarn through holes on tab; tie in a bow around handle. ◆

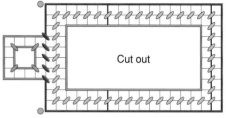

Christmas Bag Gift Tag
21 holes x 10 holes
Cut 2

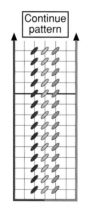

Christmas Bag Handle
6 holes x 74 holes
Cut 2

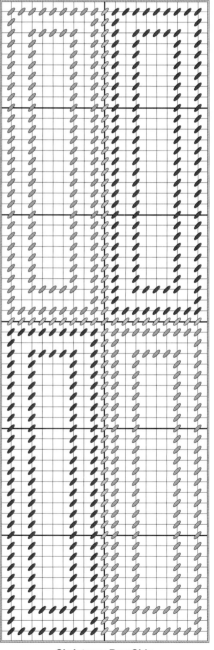

Christmas Bag Side
20 holes x 60 holes
Cut 2

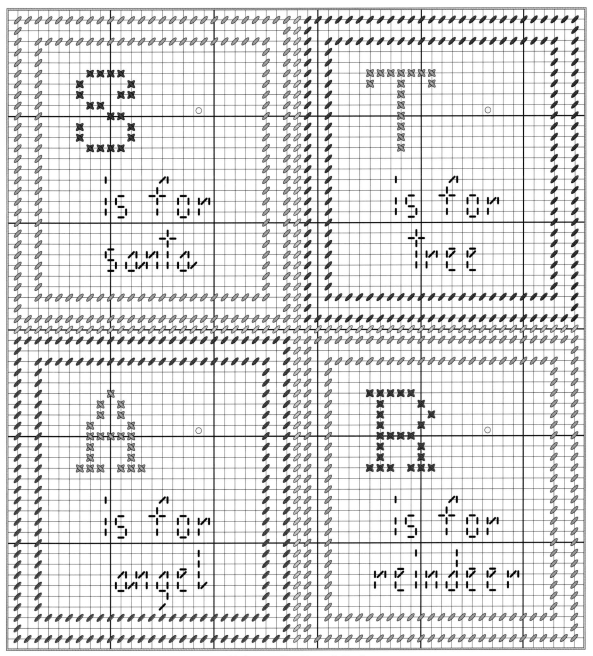

Christmas Bag Front & Back
56 holes x 60 holes
Cut 2

Summer's Day Gift Bags

Designs by Celia Lange Designs

These lovely gift bags are small in size, making them just right for many gifts we share.

Skill Level
Intermediate

GARDEN GATE BAG

Materials
- *1 sheet Darice Ultra Stiff 7-count plastic canvas*
- *Red Heart Classic worsted weight yarn Art. E267 as listed in color key*
- *Red Heart Super Saver worsted weight yarn Art. E301 as listed in color key*
- *#16 tapestry needle*
- *Assorted small silk flowers and leaves*
- *32" coordinating rayon cord*
- *Low-temperature glue gun*

Instructions
1. Cut plastic canvas according to graphs (right and page 170). Cut one 36-hole x 18-hole piece for bag bottom.

2. Stitch bottom with paddy green Continental Stitches. Stitch remaining pieces following graphs, working uncoded areas with blue jewel Continental Stitches.

3. Work French Knots and Backstitches when background stitching is completed.

4. Overcast all edges of fence pieces, front gate and gift tag with white. Overcast top edges of bag front, back and sides following graphs.

5. Whipstitch front, back and sides together following graphs, then Whipstitch bottom to front, back and sides with paddy green.

6. Using photo as a guide through step 7 and making sure bottom edges are even, glue garden gate and fence sides and back to bag. Glue leaves and flowers along and behind top edges of garden gate and just around front corners of bag.

7. For handles, cut cord in half; tie

each end in a knot. Glue ends to inner corners of bag. With white yarn, tack gift tag to bag along top edge of side near bag front.

WINDOW BOX BAG

Materials
- *1 sheet Darice Ultra Stiff 7-count plastic canvas*
- *Red Heart Classic worsted weight yarn Art. E267 as listed in color key*
- *Red Heart Super Saver worsted weight yarn Art. E301 as listed in color key*
- *#16 tapestry needle*
- *Small amount white tissue paper*
- *Assorted small silk flowers*
- *32" coordinating rayon cord*
- *Low-temperature glue gun*

Instructions
1. Cut plastic canvas according to graphs (page 171). Cut one 27-hole x 17-hole piece for bag bottom, one 27-hole x 4-hole piece for window box bottom and two 4-hole x 10-hole pieces for window box sides.

2. Stitch bottom with Windsor blue Continental Stitches; stitch window box sides and bottom with white Continental Stitches. Overcast window frame with white.

3. Stitch remaining pieces following graphs, working uncoded area on tag and window box front with white Continental Stitches and working window box back with white Continental Stitches only. Work uncoded areas on bag pieces with cornmeal Continental Stitches.

4. Work Backstitches on tag and window box front when background stitching is completed; do not add Backstitches to window box back.

5. With cornmeal, Overcast top edges of bag front, back and sides. Whipstitch sides to front and back with adjacent colors, then Whipstitch front, back and sides to bottom with Windsor blue.

6. Using white throughout, Overcast top edges of window box front, back and sides. Whipstitch front and back to sides, then Whipstitch front, back and sides to bottom.

7. Using photo as a guide through step 9, glue window frame to window on bag front, then glue window box to lower portion of window and to bag.

8. Crumple tissue paper and glue in window box to help hold shape. Glue flowers in box as desired.

9. For handles, cut cord in half; tie each end in a knot. Glue ends to inner corners of bag. With white yarn, tack gift tag to bag along top edge of side near bag front. ◆

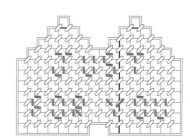

Garden Gate Bag Gift Tag
16 holes x 11 holes
Cut 1

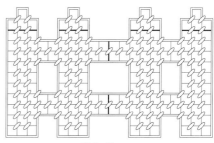

Side Fence
20 holes x 12 holes
Cut 2

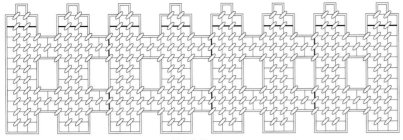

Back Fence
38 holes x 12 holes
Cut 1

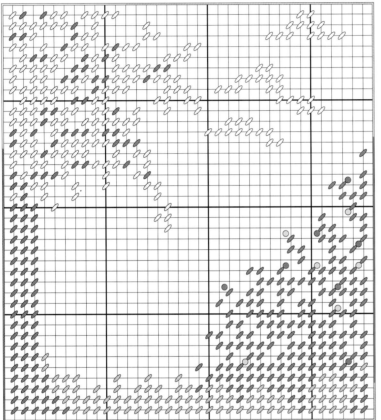

Garden Gate Front & Back
36 holes x 39 holes
Cut 2

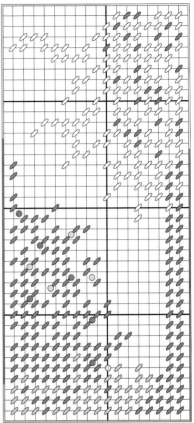

Garden Gate Bag Side
18 holes x 39 holes
Cut 2

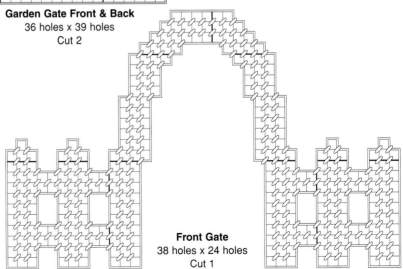

Front Gate
38 holes x 24 holes
Cut 1

COLOR KEY	
GARDEN GATE BAG	
Worsted Weight Yarn	**Yards**
☐ White #311	36
■ Mid brown #339	15
■ Hunter green #389	23
☐ Medium sage #632	18
▨ Paddy green #686	25
Uncoded areas are blue jewel #818 Continental Stitches	54
✎ Blue jewel #818 Overcasting and Whipstitching	
✎ Hunter green #389 Backstitch	
○ Rose pink #372 French Knot	2
● Country rose #374 French Knot	2

Color numbers given are for Red Heart Classic worsted weight yarn Art. E267 and Red Heart Super Saver worsted weight yarn Art. E301.

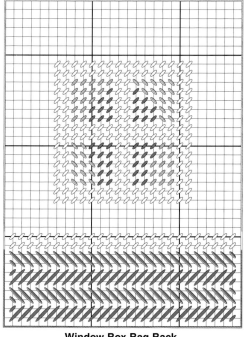

Window Box Bag Back
27 holes x 36 holes
Cut 1

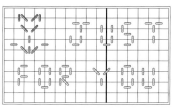

Window Box Bag Gift Tag
16 holes x 9 holes
Cut 1

Window Frame
23 holes x 25 holes
Cut 1
Do not stitch

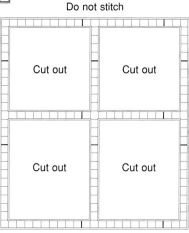

Cut out   Cut out

Cut out   Cut out

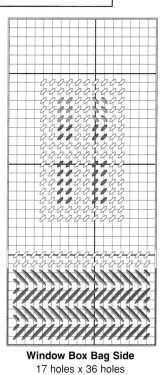

Window Box Bag Side
17 holes x 36 holes
Cut 1

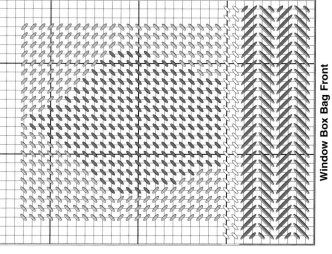

Window Box Bag Front
27 holes x 36 holes
Cut 1

Window Box Front & Back
27 holes x 10 holes
Cut 2
Stitch front as graphed
Stitch back with white Continental Stitches only

Skill Level
Beginner

Materials
- 1½ sheets 10-count plastic canvas
- DMC 6-strand embroidery floss as listed in color key
- #22 tapestry needle
- 2 sheets black felt
- 36" black satin cord or satin ribbon
- White glue

Project Note
Use 12 strands floss for all stitching.

Instructions
1. Cut plastic canvas according to graphs. Cut one 73-hole x 64-hole piece for bag back, two 25-hole x 64-hole pieces for bag sides and one 73-hole x 25-hole piece for bag bottom. Bag bottom will remain unstitched.

2. Cut one piece of felt each for

COLOR KEY	
6-Strand Embroidery Floss	**Yards**
◢ Black #310	157
◢ Christmas red #321	2
⬭ Very dark rose #326	2
⬭ Rose #335	3
⬭ Light pistachio green #368	5
⬭ Dark blue green #501	5
◇ Medium blue green #503	18
⬭ Light blue green #504	4
⬭ Light tangerine #742	1
⬯ Medium yellow #743	2
☆ Light pale yellow #745	2
▽ Medium pink #776	2
◆ Dark garnet #814	2
■ Garnet #816	4
⬭ Medium rose #899	2
✦ Light khaki green #3013	4
◢ Dark mauve #3685	2
▼ Mauve #3687	2
⬭ Medium mauve #3688	2
⬯ Light mauve #3689	2
⬭ Medium melon #3706	2
◆ Light Christmas red #3801	3
⬯ Ultra pale yellow #3823	2
Color numbers given are for DMC 6-strand embroidery floss.	

Floral Fantasy Bag

Design by Kathleen Marie O'Donnell

Perfect for Mother's Day, anniversaries or many other special occasions, this lovely gift bag is rich with elegance and fine taste!

bag front, back and both sides and two pieces of felt for bag bottom, cutting felt slightly smaller all around than matching plastic canvas piece.

3. Following graph, Continental Stitch design on bag front, then work black background with vertical Slanting Gobelin Stitches over two bars, working compensating stitches around design over one bar where necessary.

4. For back, work vertical columns of Slanting Gobelin Stitches over two bars. Work side pieces in vertical columns of Slanting Gobelin Stitches over four bars.

5. Glue felt to backside of side pieces. For handle, cut satin cord in half. Lay felt on wrong sides of front and back; place cord ends between bag and felt along side edges, making sure handle loops are equal length. Glue felt and cord in place, using extra glue if necessary to secure cord ends.

6. Using black throughout, Overcast top edges of bag pieces. Whipstitch sides to front and back; Whipstitch bottom to front, back and sides.

7. Glue one piece of felt to both sides of bag bottom. ◆

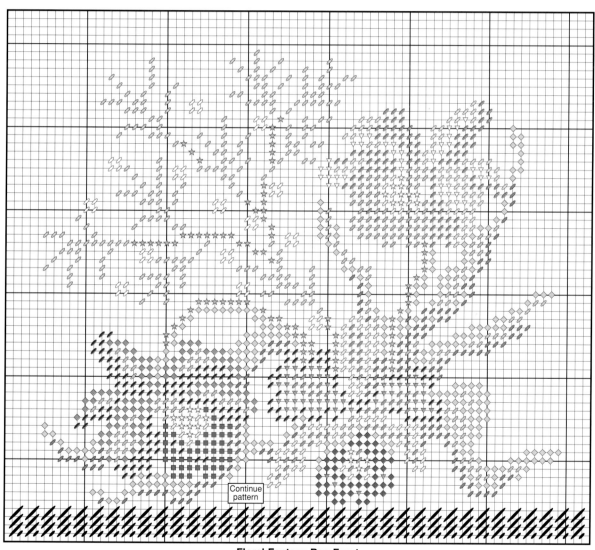

Floral Fantasy Bag Front
73 holes x 64 holes
Cut 1

Stitch Guide

Use the following diagrams to expand your plastic canvas stitching. For each diagram, bring needle up through canvas at the red number one and go back down through the canvas at the red number two. The second stitch is numbered in green. Always bring needle up through the canvas at odd numbers and take it back down through the canvas at the even numbers.

Background Stitches

The following stitches are used for filling in large areas of canvas. The Continental Stitch is the most commonly used stitch. Other stitches, such as the Condensed Mosaic and Scotch Stitch, fill in large areas of canvas more quickly than the Continental Stitch because their stitches cover a larger area of canvas.

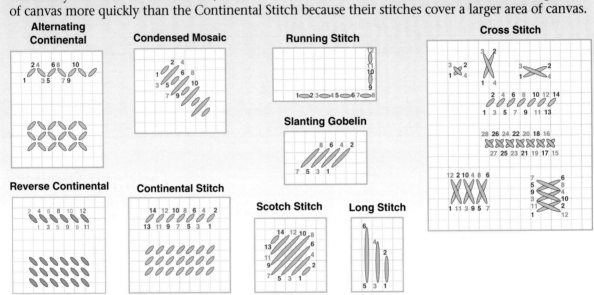

Embroidery Stitches

Embroidery stitches are worked on top of a stitched area to add detail and beauty to your project. Embroidery stitches are usually worked with one strand of yarn, several strands of pearl cotton or several strands of embroidery floss.

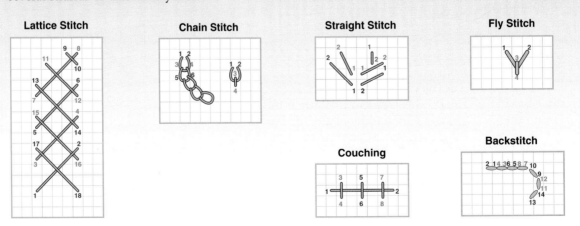

Embroidery Stitches

French Knot

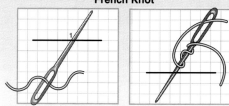

Bring needle up through piece.

Wrap yarn around needle 2 or 3 times, depending on desired size of knot; take needle back through piece through same hole.

Lazy Daisy

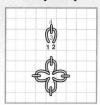

Bring yarn needle up through canvas, then back down in same hole, leaving a small loop.

Then, bring needle up inside loop; take needle back down through piece on other side of loop.

Specialty Stitches

The following stitches can be worked either on top of a previously stitched area or directly onto the canvas. Like the embroidery stitches, these too add wonderful detail and give your stitching additional interest and texture.

Diamond Eyelet

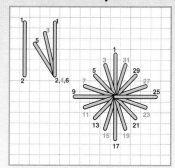

For each stitch, bring needle up at odd numbers around outside and take needle down through canvas at center hole.

Smyrna Cross

Satin Stitch

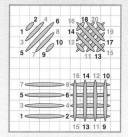

This stitch gives a "padded" look to your work.

Finishing Stitches

Both of these stitches are used to finish the outer edges of the canvas. Overcasting is done to finish one edge at a time. Whipstitch is used to stitch two pieces of canvas together. For both Overcasting and Whipstitching, work one stitch in each hole along straight edges and inside corners, and two or three stitches in outside corners.

Overcast/Whipstitch

Loop Stitch or Turkey Loop Stitch

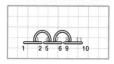

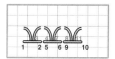

The top diagram shows this stitch left intact. This is an effective stitch for giving a project dimensional hair. The bottom diagram demonstrates the cut loop stitch. Because each stitch is anchored, cutting it will not cause the stitches to come out. A group of cut loop stitches gives a fluffy, soft look and feel to your project.

Special Thanks

We would like to give special thanks and acknowledgment to the following designers whose work is published in this book.

Angie Arickx
Fancy Hearts Vanity Set, Log Cabin Tissue Topper, Stitchin' Caddy

Vicki Blizzard
A Furry Little Christmas; Angelic Music Box; Baby's First Christmas Ornament; Busy Bee Bookmark; Delightful Daisy Musical Magnet; Doggie Treats Jar; Fancy Frames; Fishy Frame; In the Doghouse Frame; Kitty Toys; Garage Bookends; Pearled Hearts Basket; Pet Leash Hanger; Quick Stitch Cat Collars; Singing Birdhouse Magnet; The Queen's Crown & Jewels; Tiny Treasures Music Box; Triple Photo Frame; Veggie Jar Tags; Way Cool Magnets

Celia Lange & Martha Bleidner of Celia Lange Designs
A Starry Christmas Bag, Birdhouse Photo Frame, Bridal Suite Door Hanger, Country Plaid Recipe Card Box, Father's Blessing Sampler, Nature's Majesty Frame, Summer's Day Gift Bags

Ronda Bryce
Primary Colors Gift Box, Southwest Pencil Holders, Tepee Bank

Mary T. Cosgrove
Cash Register, Garden Fridgies, Grandma's Pride & Joy, Ice Cream Cone Key Ring, Office Message Center

Darla J. Fanton
Love & Dreams

Lilo Fruehwirth
Pastel Treasures

Janelle Giese
Lucky Duck Gift Caddy, Teddy Bear Picnic

Joan Green
Bargello Jewel Box, Bright Checks Diaper Dispenser, Kitchen Cottage, Potpourri Birdhouse

Johnna Miller
Old MacDonald's Farm

Carol Nartowicz
Chrysanthemum Organizer, Embossed Flowers Ensemble, On Par Frame

Kathleen Marie O'Donnell
Floral Fantasy Bag

Terry Ricioli
Lovebirds

Niki Russos-Atkinson
Catch of the Day Coaster Set, Fiesta Table Set

Laura Scott
Pretty Pastels Gift Boxes

Kimberly A. Suber
Baby's First Frame, Sunny Sunflower Tote

Ruby Thacker
Medals of Honor Desk Set

Michele Wilcox
Cottage Doorstop, Kissing in a Tree, Sisters Are Forever

Linda Wyszynski
Birdhouse Coaster Set

Louise Young
The Littlest Doghouse

Buyer's Guide

The Beadery Craft Products
105 Canonchet Rd.
P.O. Box 178
Hope Valley, RI 02832
(401) 539-2432

Blumenthal Lansing Co.
1929 Main St.
Lansing, IA 52151
(800) 553-4158

Coats & Clark
P.O. Box 12229
Greenville, SC 26912-0229
(800) 648-1479
www.coatsandclark.com

C.W. Fifield Co. Inc.
4 Keith Way
Kingham, MA 02043-4202
(617) 749-6357

Darice mail order source:
Bolek's
330 N. Tuscarawas Ave.
Dover, OH 44622
(330) 364-8878

DecoArt
P.O. Box 360
Stanford, KY 40484
(800) 367-3047

Delta
2550 Pellissier Pl.
Whittier, CA 90601
(800) 423-4135

The DMC Corp.
10 Port Kearny
South Kearny, NJ 07032
(800) 275-4117

Forster Inc.
P.O. Box 657
Wilton, ME 04294-0657
(207) 645-2574

Gay Bowles Sales Inc.
P.O. Box 1060
Janesville, WI 53547
(800) 447-1332

JHB International Inc.
1955 S. Quince St.
Denver, CO 90746
(303) 715-3030

Kreinik Mfg. Co. Inc.
3106 Timanus Ln., #101
Baltimore, MD 21244
(410) 281-0040

Kunin Felt Co./Foss Mfg. Co. Inc.
380 Lafayette Rd.
P.O. Box 5000
Hampton, NH 03842
(800) 292-7900

Madeira
SCS
9631 N.E. Colfax St.
Portland, OR 97220-1232
(800) 542-4727

National Artcraft Co.
7996 Darrow Rd.
Twinsburg, OH 44087
(888) 937-2723

One & Only Creations
P.O. Box 2730
Napa, CA 94558
(800) 262-6768

Rainbow Gallery
mail order source:
Designs by Joan Green
1130 Tollgate Drive
Oxford, OH 45056
(513) 523-2690

Rhode Island Textile Co.
P.O. Box 999
Pawtucket, RI 02862
(401) 722-3700

Spinrite Inc.
Box 40
Listowel, Ontario
Canada N4W 3H3
(519) 291-3780

Therm O Web
770 Glenn Ave.
Wheeling, IL 60090
(847) 520-5200

Unicorn Studios
P.O. Box 9240
Knoxville, TN 37940
(800) 874-5317

Uniek mail order source:
The Needlecraft Shop
23 Old Pecan Rd.
Big Sandy, TX 75755
(800) 259-4000